DIVORCED, BEHEADED, SOLD

DIVORCED, BEHEADED, SOLD

Ending an English Marriage 1500–1847

Maria Nicolaou

PEN & SWORD
HISTORY

First published in Great Britain in 2014 by
PEN AND SWORD HISTORY
an imprint of
Pen and Sword Books Ltd
47 Church Street
Barnsley
South Yorkshire S70 2AS

ISBN 978 1 78159 340 0

Printed and bound in England
by CPI Group (UK) Ltd, Croydon, CR0 4YY

Typeset in Times New Roman by
CHIC GRAPHICS

Pen & Sword Books Ltd incorporates the imprints of Pen & Sword
Archaeology, Atlas, Aviation, Battleground, Discovery, Family
History, History, Maritime, Military, Naval, Politics, Railways, Select,
Social History, Transport, True Crime, and Claymore Press, Frontline
Books, Leo Cooper, Praetorian Press, Remember When, Seaforth
Publishing and Wharncliffe.

For a complete list of Pen and Sword titles please contact
Pen and Sword Books Limited
47 Church Street, Barnsley, South Yorkshire, S70 2AS, England
E-mail: enquiries@pen-and-sword.co.uk
Website: www.pen-and-sword.co.uk

Contents

Acknowledgements

So many people have assisted me in this journey that it is difficult to know where to begin. From the start, I have been supported by my capable and efficient editor, Jennifer Newby. I am exceedingly grateful, not only for her insightful comments and suggestions, but also for her enthusiasm about this project. I am obliged to my publishers, Pen and Sword, for giving me the opportunity to write this book.

It is impossible to overstate how grateful I am to one of my former lecturers, Professor Bernard Capp, who first suggested to me that marital separation was a potential topic of investigation, and how it could be researched. I would never have considered this topic possible without him. My sincere thanks go to him for his help and guidance over the years. I am similarly grateful to my former supervisor, Professor Beat Kümin. Professor Kümin read over drafts of the dissertation on which this book was based, and provided many helpful hints as to sources and how marital breakdown fitted into the early modern world at large. Ms Joanna Kemp assisted me by translating a Latin appendix to Wriothesley's *Chronicle*.

The works of Lawrence Stone not only gave me a general introduction to the period, but also led me to some of the most well-documented cases of marital breakdown. I have looked at several of the same cases as Stone, although my interpretation of the primary sources tends to vary slightly, most notably with the case of Lady Westmeath. Similarly, Samuel Menefee provided a useful list of wife sale cases, which greatly assisted my own research.

Several bodies very kindly gave their permission for me to quote from their documents. The Parliamentary Archives gave me permission to quote from their documents on parliamentary divorce, and the trustees of Lambeth Palace allowed me to quote from the

ACKNOWLEDGEMENTS

records of the Court of Arches. The National Archives allowed me to quote from the records of the Court of Requests. The Trustees of the British Library permitted me to quote from the Althorp Papers, the letters of the Duchess of Kingston to Lord Barrington, the correspondence of Elizabeth and Anthony Bourne, and letters of the Duchess of Devonshire to Lady Melbourne. The Marquess of Salisbury very kindly allowed me to access and quote the papers of the Marchioness of Westmeath at Hatfield House. The University of Leicester permitted me to quote from the records of the Old Bailey. Cambridge University Press and Merlin Press have allowed me to quote from various publications.

CHAPTER 1

The World of Marriage

In 1566, Thomas Burgess walks out of the humble dwelling that he shares with his wife Joan without a word, never to return. In 1636, Elizabeth Norris does not celebrate Easter with a carefree heart. She has just received the news that her husband has not only stolen her property but has maliciously had their marriage declared invalid on the grounds of bigamy. In the summer of 1768, the Duke of Grafton reads a letter from his agent, telling him that the spies he has planted in the house of his estranged wife will soon provide proof of her illegitimate child, allowing him to obtain a divorce. These couples were divided from each other by time, geography and social status. Nevertheless, they all had one thing in common: their marriages had collapsed in early modern England.

Today, most people assume that divorce is a relatively modern invention. We read *Jane Eyre* and hear that Mr Rochester is irrevocably bound to his insane wife, leaving him no choice but to marry Jane bigamously. We watch *Pride and Prejudice* and see Mr and Mrs Bennet sniping at each other, trapped in a marriage that Austen describes as devoid of 'real affection... not... a very pleasing picture of conjugal felicity or domestic comfort'. The film *The Duchess* paints a dire portrait of life after divorce, where Georgiana, Duchess of Devonshire, is faced with the prospect of losing her children, income and social position – in short, her world.

This, combined with twenty-first century reports on ever-increasing divorce rates, leaves people believing that before our modern day, marital break-ups were almost non-existent. The all-powerful forces of religion, money and society meant that women in particular needed to put up and shut up with miserable marriages. This, however, was simply not always true. Not only were there separations but women could also, in some cases, walk away from their marriages with more than would be expected. In *Divorced, Beheaded, Sold*, we will meet those who were determined to defy convention and who succeeded in escaping their marriages.

Before we start exploring the worlds and lives of these men and women we need to understand more about the societies they lived in, and what marriage and separation would have meant to them. The world of a sixteenth century woman would have differed greatly from that of a nineteenth century lady. Throughout this book we will pass from the realm of Henry VIII to that of Queen Victoria. The sixteenth century is clearly linked to the medieval era, while the nineteenth century is more obviously recognisable as the forerunner of our modern world.

In 1500, church services were considered an effective cure for the plague outbreaks that regularly killed thousands; America had not yet been discovered; the King's will was paramount and Parliament was merely a vehicle that monarchs could command, as Henry VIII would do during his infamous marital escapades. Yet by 1847, both the Industrial and Scientific revolutions had taken place; the British Empire was expanding; and Parliament had overseen the murder of Charles I and the formation of a republic. Although the monarchy had been restored, the Catholic Stuarts had long since been replaced with their distant relatives, the Hanoverians, and, while Queen Victoria governed the United Kingdom, she did so firmly in conjunction with Parliament.

All these numerous changes meant that men and women's options when it came to freeing themselves from an unwanted marriage would fluctuate over the centuries. A woman marrying in the 1500s lived in a very different world and would have faced starkly different options to her nineteenth century counterparts. Similarly, the vast inequalities between the lives of the poor, the prosperous and the very rich meant that they would take very different routes when it came to marriage and separation.

DIVORCED, BEHEADED, SOLD

As we know, the 1500s were anchored firmly in the medieval era. England's first sixteenth century monarch, Henry VII, won his throne by right of conquest, ending the Wars of the Roses and changing England's ruling dynasty from Plantagenet to Tudor. His son and successor, Henry VIII, is one of the best examples history has to offer of a despotic, autocratic king. In Tudor England his personal wishes were decrees, most memorably his desire to marry Anne Boleyn. Aspiring Tudor politicians, hungry for power and wealth, sought not to gain a seat in Parliament but to gain access to the King in a bid to win his favour and influence policy through him. There was 'rampant competition'[1] for places in the Privy Chamber, close to the King. One of the most prestigious positions, ridiculous though it may seem to us, was the Groom of the Stool, who obtained his prestige through his close position to the King, attending to his bathroom requirements and accompanying him to the toilet when the need arose. The ability to enter the King's bedchamber uninvited, so giving him unparalleled access to the monarch, was of paramount importance in a time when the King's word was law and there were no checks upon his power.

At this time, women could play a political role through promoting either their families or powerful factions at court. Young women of high social status were sent by ambitious relatives to the court, either to make a good marriage or to gain a political role through becoming the King's mistress. The use of women to forge and solidify political alliances intensified when Henry became adamant that he would have his marriage to Katherine of Aragon annulled, despite the numerous political problems it caused. This desire for a divorce was partly due to Henry wanting a male heir, but also largely because Henry had decided that his future lay with Anne Boleyn. Similarly, he showed no hesitation in later annulling his marriage to Anne of Cleves, even though it would destroy the Protestant alliance he had made with her brother, the Duke of Cleves.

Women at court were now not only aiming to attract the King and gain as much advancement for their families as possible before his interest waned, but also hoping to become an officially recognised wife. Anne Boleyn was replaced by Jane Seymour, who belonged to a political faction hostile to the Boleyns, while Anne of Cleves, whose marriage had been promoted by Thomas Cromwell, was replaced by Katherine Howard, niece to the Duke of Norfolk. At a time when politics and power were so intensely personal, women could and did play significant roles in determining England's future.

Things began to change, however, with the accession of Charles I in 1625. Charles' characteristic inability to negotiate or compromise in political and religious matters may have been reminiscent of Henry VIII, but it also led him into clashes with a Parliament that was becoming increasingly determined to play a significant role in England's government. These disputes culminated with the English Civil War and Charles' execution on 30 January 1649. For the first time in the country's history, England was a republic. The days of personal rule were over. Women were no longer flocking to court in order to play a political role, but those of both low and high status gained increased independence by running estates and farms, while their husbands and/or fathers were engaging in military action.

Even though the Republic was short-lived, with the monarchy restored in 1660 after the death of Oliver Cromwell, it was a powerful reminder to both the monarchy and the people alike that Kings and Queens could be deposed if they refused to listen to the populace. This did, in fact, happen in 1688 when James II refused to take account of popular anxiety about his Catholicism. Consequently, he was replaced by his son-in-law and daughter, William III and Mary II. Later, Parliament stepped in again to invite the Hanoverians to rule Great Britain. After the Protestant Stuarts died out in 1714 with the death of Queen Anne, Parliament preferred to choose their monarch from the Protestant descendants of Princess Elizabeth, who had left England more than 100 years earlier, rather than call back the logical heir, James II's son, James Francis Stuart, from exile.

These events reminded people that the monarch was no longer believed to rule solely by the will of God, but also by the will of Parliament and the people. While women still aimed to make a good match, this was mainly for personal and familial advancement, and not for political reasons. Women who wished to exert political power now attempted to influence the Parliamentary process. Georgiana, Duchess of Devonshire, famously used her social position and wealth to campaign for the Whigs. Monarchs could no longer govern solely as they wished. When George IV came under pressure to marry and father an heir, he was not able to acknowledge his first wife, Maria Fitzherbert, openly, owing to her Catholic religion. When he later attempted to divorce his publicly recognised wife, Queen Caroline, he was prevented from doing so by the strength of public opinion, despite proof of her adultery.

There was a tremendous uproar in 1839 (the so-called 'Bedchamber crisis') when Queen Victoria took steps to ensure that her then favourite Prime Minister, Viscount Melbourne, continued in office, despite the fact that Robert Peel's party had obtained the most votes in the recent election. While this move would have been expected in the sixteenth or even seventeenth centuries, it was not acceptable in the nineteenth. The resulting public outrage and demonstrations meant that no other monarch ever attempted to influence politics publicly again. The monarch had evolved from possessing absolute power to the figurehead monarch we have today. The growing belief that ordinary people had the right to choose their own rulers led to the formation of movements such as Chartism. The Chartists campaigned for the vote to be extended to all men and for various parliamentary reforms which would increase the numbers of voters and give more men the chance of standing for Parliament. Although the system was not yet fully democratic in 1849, it was recognisable as the forerunner of the parliamentary democracy we know today.

Other significant changes occurred in people's attitudes towards religion and the supernatural. In 1500, Catholicism lay at the heart of people's lives. The Church, governed from Rome, in theory controlled every element of people's lives, from their behaviour to when they married, and even what people ate and when. The Church had its own courts, commonly known as 'Bawdy Courts' because many of the accusations and testimonies made there were of a sexual nature. Women could be, and frequently were, prosecuted and sentenced for offences ranging from simply not attending church, to illicit affairs.

Yet, women could themselves initiate prosecutions in the Church Courts and they played a role in the story of women's attempts to liberate themselves from unhappy marriages.

In the 1530s religion was, quite literally, a matter of life and death. Henry VIII's decision to break away from Catholicism meant that Christianity in England entered a period of turbulence. Despite having used Protestant beliefs to justify ending the Pope's authority, Henry wished to retain Catholic forms of worship. This was followed by the contradictory short reigns of Edward VI, who made far-reaching moves to convert the English to Protestantism, and Mary I, an almost fanatical Catholic who believed that her failure to have a child could be remedied by burning Protestants to death.

Over a 25-year period, England had gone through approximately four official religion changes, seesawing between Protestantism and Catholicism. This led to a terrifying situation where people could be persecuted as heretics either for being too Catholic and supporting the restoration of the Pope's authority, or for being too Protestant and supporting further religious reforms. Practically anyone could be charged as a heretic during the Tudor era. Even Katherine Parr, the last wife of Henry VIII, came close to being arrested and imprisoned for supporting proposed reforms that Henry saw as overly Protestant.

One particularly horrifying case was that of Perrotine Massey, a pregnant woman who was burnt to death with her mother and sister during the reign of Mary I. Their neighbour had maliciously accused them of heresy after they revealed he was guilty of theft. Perrotine gave birth while she was tied to the stake. The baby was initially pulled out of the fire but then thrown back on the orders of the local sheriff. These were dangerous times for all women, but it can be argued that women's expected devotion to religion made them increasingly vulnerable to accusations of heresy.

Although heresy prosecutions ended with the Tudor dynasty, religious tensions continued until well into the Restoration. Although England was comparatively peaceful during the eighteenth century, Catholics were still subject to a series of discriminatory laws which prohibited them from becoming involved in public life, including holding political office. Even though these laws were gradually repealed – such as the 1778 Catholic Relief Act, which allowed Catholics to join the army – full religious toleration only occurred in 1829, when the Duke of Wellington, spurred on by radically decreasing levels of adherence to religion and anti-Catholicism, repealed all anti-Catholic laws.

The Bawdy Courts were largely officially abolished in the late 1700s. Their inability to imprison people and their other weak punishments meant that they became increasingly irrelevant in a world where the Church's formal power was decreasing. It is worth bearing in mind that, depending on the lady's personal circumstances and the religious changes then taking place, religion would impact on couples in different ways and to different extents, depending on what century they were living in.

The loosening of religious restrictions was part of a growing trend of secularisation, which started in the eighteenth century and quickly gathered force. In the sixteenth century, the existence of magic, divination and astrology was still seen as an indisputable fact. Many chose to resort to 'white' magic to try and guarantee their own wellbeing, or simply a good harvest. Royal courts had their own official astrologers, such as Elizabeth I's astrologer, John Dee. The Devil was seen to be at work everywhere, usually through witches. When Henry VIII wished to discredit his wife, Anne Boleyn, one of the accusations made was that she was a witch. James I gave further official backing to the existence of witches in his 1597 work *Daemonologie*.

England did not experience the same witchcraft hysteria as did parts of continental Europe and Scotland, yet it was not without its persecutions. Women in sixteenth and seventeenth century England had to be wary of indulging in behaviour that could lead them to be accused of witchcraft. Although this might result in increased respect within the community, granting them a degree of protection from unscrupulous individuals, it could also lead to execution. One of the most well-known persecutions was the case of the Pendle Hill witches, where nine out of the eleven accused, ten of whom were women, were prosecuted for witchcraft at the Assizes. Only one young girl was acquitted, leaving the rest to be executed by hanging. The most notable series of English witchcraft persecutions came in the 1640s, when Matthew Hopkins took advantage of the political turmoil caused by the Civil War to start witchcraft trials in Essex, leading to the death of an estimated 300 women.[2] Those living alone were particularly vulnerable to accusations of witchcraft, meaning that separated women were perhaps more at risk than others.

Men and women whose stories are discussed within this book would place differing emphasis on science and religion, depending on the era in which they lived. Religion slowly began to share ground with scientific influences. The Scientific Revolution gave birth to a wave of experiments that disproved traditional thinking and paved the way for new influences, such as Copernicus, who disproved the then commonly accepted theory that the sun revolved around the earth. Meanwhile English scientist Isaac Newton famously solved 'the puzzle of the force of gravity'.[3] These new findings gave science an enhanced place in society and led people to place a new importance on science and facts. Dogmatism and beliefs regarding supernatural phenomenon such as witches gradually waned and became old-fashioned.

While religion remained an important and significant part of people's lives, it had to share its power with competing forces. These influences culminated in the eighteenth century, when the Enlightenment movement reached its epoque and it became fashionable to challenge traditional thinking and 'superstition'. Instead followers placed their faith in rationalism, science and logic.

Ordinary people's lives were also drastically affected by the numerous technological advances taking place. Inventions such as the printing press meant that books no longer had to be slowly written out by hand. From the 1440s books could be produced relatively cheaply and quickly in large quantities. The increasing amount of accessible print material meant that more people were learning to read. The cheap price of ballads and pamphlets meant that stories or information could be spread wide, making popular unrest and dissatisfaction more likely. It seems probable that this increase in literacy may also have left people more informed and able to access legal resources and end their marriages.

A growing need for information and the collapse of censorship meant that early newspapers, news-books, began to be published in the 1640s. One of the first newspapers, *The London Gazette,* was published in 1665. By the nineteenth century, there were more than 50 newspapers in London alone, including *The Times*. Some of the couples featured in this book found that their marriages and affairs were discussed publicly in these newspapers.

The economy also underwent dramatic changes throughout the period we explore within these pages. Technological improvements meant that the first industries began to develop, with women playing a role in the cloth and silk industries through home-based work such as spinning and weaving. These developments led to the Industrial Revolution, which left no corner of people's lives untouched. The introduction of new machines led to the growth of factories, which became an increasingly important source of employment. People migrated to areas where factories were concentrated, leading to the growth of existing and new cities. This settlement in unprecedented numbers led to a wide variety of social changes. Some women were able to find employment outside of the home in factories, giving them increased independence.

People's perceptions and beliefs regarding the wider world also changed dramatically over the centuries. In the 1500s, the average man and woman would have had a limited knowledge of the world beyond Europe. The Americas, for example, were largely unknown. Over the next 300 years, major efforts would be made to find new territories and establish control over them. Companies such as the East India Company were set up to help Britain gain influence over India, and a share of its wealth. By the nineteenth century, this had expanded into a global empire. Some of the women whom we will encounter were not only fleeing their husbands, but also a life in the colonies. The development of the slave trade aided Britain's economic boom, leading to employment opportunities for lower class women and increased power for women in the higher sections of society, who acted as principal consumers.

16

One of the most important social changes in our story is how the perception of women altered throughout the centuries. Women's subordination remained constant. English society was patriarchal and male authority was supported both within the family and society at large. The common perception of and general attitudes towards women, however, changed dramatically. In Tudor England, women were seen as an imperfect version of men. Bodies were believed to be made up of 'humours', the balance of which was seen as responsible for determining a person's gender and personality. The balance of these humours believed necessary for a foetus to become female was also thought to make the developing foetus 'intellectually, morally and physically weaker'.[4] Women were therefore automatically seen as a more stupid and immoral version of men. These beliefs led to books such as John Knox's *The Monstrous Regiment of Women*, which argues that female power was 'repugnant to nature'.

Yet as these beliefs changed, so did general attitudes towards women. By the eighteenth century women were seen increasingly as being a completely separate sex from men, as frail and in need of male protection, not control, and society's view of acceptable behaviour in marriage changed greatly. Violence towards women was still practised, yet it was no longer as acceptable as it had once been. In 1846, *The Times* complained that 'the conjugal tie appears to be considered as conferring on the man a certain degree of impunity for brutality towards the woman', and historian Elizabeth Foyster has linked the rise of wives being imprisoned in lunatic asylums to an increased societal antipathy towards wife-beating.

Marriages and separations were, for most of the early modern period, not subject to the same controls and regulations as today. We now have a very specific image of what form a wedding ceremony must take in order for it to be recognised as a valid marriage. We expect that ceremonies will be conducted by a state official, who today could be a registrar but in the past would have been a vicar. We also expect that there will be some kind of official paperwork to certify that a marriage has taken place, such as a certificate and/or an entry in the church registers, and that at least two witnesses will normally be present.

When couples asked themselves, 'Where shall we get married?' a church ceremony was not their only option. Two 'culturally acceptable forms of marriage in England' existed from the Middle Ages until 1753.[5] One of these was the 'official' form that we would recognise today: a public ceremony conducted within a church by an ordained vicar. This would also have followed rules regarding banns, which was a public announcement in church that couples intended to marry, or licences, which overcame this requirement and could be purchased from the church. The gentry and aristocracy invariably adopted this method, but couples from lower down the social scale faced a greater range of options. Secondly, there were also other, lesser known forms, which were fairly popular with young couples.

The lack of government control over marriage ceremonies meant that a variety of popular, unofficial marriage rituals flourished, especially with couples who were either unwilling or unable to submit themselves to official rituals. One semi-official marriage ritual was known as a 'contract marriage'. From the thirteenth century onwards, the Pope decreed that the only requirement for a recognised marriage was the consent of both spouses. This opened the door for couples to form their own betrothal/marital contracts, independent of the Church. Sometimes, tokens, such as coins, would be exchanged to try and add an element of formality to the process. In 1652, one man attempted to prove a contract marriage had taken place by the acceptance of a ring inscribed in Latin 'Whom God hath joined, let no man put asunder'.

Most contracts were completely verbal. This led to a minefield of ambiguous situations. The rules of marriage contract ceremonies were complex and many did not fully understand them. For example, simply saying: 'I take you for my husband/wife', was a valid marriage in itself, and was as equally binding as a church ceremony. Anyone attempting to marry afterwards, therefore, was doing so bigamously. The declaration: 'I shall take you for my husband/wife', though, was not a binding commitment, unless it was followed by sexual intercourse. Similarly, contracts which stated, 'I will marry you, if your parents consent/provide me with a dowry of £100', would have been similarly conditional. This could lead to a range of confusing and difficult situations, where one party could claim that he and the other party had exchanged binding vows in private and that consequently they were married. This was used by a variety of people who wished to force fathers to fulfil their obligations or simply exact revenge on a former fiancé(e).

On the other hand, genuine cases were often difficult to prove, leaving unhappy spouses free to claim that they had 'accidentally' used the wrong version of vows and that they were consequently unmarried, despite having lived together as man and wife. The private nature of these contracts made it easy for people to live together as a married couple, even though they may not have been legally married. If a couple cohabited together, used the same surname and baptised their children in the manner of a legally married couple, they would have been accepted by the community as a married couple.

Complex cases, as well as the Church's desire to gain more control over marriages, led to the Church becoming increasingly hostile to contract marriages. They enforced contracts with decreasing regularity, refusing to break up subsequent marriages celebrated in church and ordering people to cease claiming marriages based on verbal contracts. Young couples, either unwilling or unable to undergo formal marriage ceremonies would, however, continue to take advantage of the lack of official control.

Another semi-official marriage ritual was that of clandestine marriages. Clandestine marriages were those which had been conducted in a way that followed enough of the church rules to still be legally binding. They followed the ritual laid out in the official *Book of Common Prayer,* and were usually performed by a man who had at some time been ordained, even if he was no longer a clergyman. They were most often performed in secret, without the reading of banns or the purchase of a licence. They would not have been recorded in the official parish register but in a private registry held by the clergyman, or not at all. They might have taken place in a parish church but they were more likely to take place elsewhere: in a 'Peculiar', a church that had accidentally fallen outside of official control; a tavern; a private home; even a brothel.

Clandestine marriages became increasingly popular as contract marriages declined in popularity. The presence of a clergyman and the use of the Church's ceremony made the ceremony seem formal and binding. The Interregnum's temporary abolition of Church marriages between 1640 and 1660 meant that those couples who wished to be married by a clergyman had no choice but to marry clandestinely.

Couples who married clandestinely usually did so to conceal a pregnancy out of wedlock, or were under the age of 21, perhaps fearing family opposition or dismissal from employment or apprenticeships. Some simply wanted to avoid *charivaris*, which were noisy parades intended to express community disapproval of a forthcoming marriage. A few were plotting scams. Con Philips, who we shall encounter later in this book, married a professional bridegroom in an elaborate plot to escape imprisonment for her debts. Their convenience made clandestine marriages very popular. In the late 1600s, the three most famous 'Peculiar' churches in London conducted 2,500-3,000 marriages a year, which was nearly the equivalent of the total of official marriages in all of London.

This state of affairs did not last forever. After 1753, Hardwicke's Marriage Act ensured that there would be no legal recognition of any marriage not performed and recorded in a parish church by a recognised clergyman and at least two witnesses. Ministers who conducted a marriage outside the boundaries of this act could be punished with transportation.

The method that a couple had chosen to marry would impact greatly on the way they chose to separate when things went wrong. This was not a world where you could walk up to the nearest court and file for divorce. Spouses, especially women, needed to think carefully about their options and decide not only which one was right for them, but how they would present themselves to others. Would they run away? Seek help from a male relative? Present themselves to a court as an innocent victim? Women's options also varied according to their social status. While women with access to money might have been able to access more legal services, they were also more likely to face stronger social prohibitions.

The further down the social scale you were, the greater the anonymity you could adopt, with many unhappy spouses simply choosing to abandon their families. A great deal depended on the personalities in question. While some people chose the commonplace, such as abandonment or legal separations, others chose more unorthodox methods, such as wife-sales. There were no hard and fast rules when it came to marital breakdown. The best way to investigate how and why couples made the choices they did, is for us, quite simply, to peek into their lives.

CHAPTER 2

Informal Separation:
From Living Asunder to
Household Captivity

'A deserted lady, or gentlewoman, is become a common notion. Now the dogs bark at the Masters of the family, when they return, as if they were absolute strangers'. Today, we assume that in the past most couples would stay together no matter what the circumstances, but according to contemporaries cases of marital breakdown and separation were numerous and frequent. Sometimes, this involved one or both partners bigamously setting up a new life with another partner. Unofficial separations can be difficult to trace. Their hidden nature means that there are few sources through which we can chart marriage breakdowns. Nevertheless, enough clues remain to reveal that informal separations occurred. Separating from one's spouse informally could be relatively easy, especially if you were a man. Although women faced greater difficulties, they too could use ingenuity and intelligence to forge a separation from their husbands and live a comfortable, independent life.

Ascertaining exactly how frequent these unofficial separations were is a difficult task, as many were unrecorded. Nevertheless, there are indications that separations were both common and well-known to early modern society and that they were a cause of official concern. There was a widespread interest in the possibility of divorce and marital separation among literate groups. John Milton, a noted philosopher, published his bestselling book, *The Doctrine and Discipline of Divorce,* towards the beginning of the English Civil War in 1643. He himself was informally separated from his wife. Milton had married a 16-year-old girl, Mary Powell, in 1642, but she had returned home to her family only one month after her marriage. The couple would later reconcile but during their period of estrangement, Milton published several pamphlets arguing not only that divorce should be legalised but also that it should be available on a no-fault basis. He argued that it was easy for marriages to disintegrate based on simple incompatibility:

> *that for all the warinesse can be us'd, it may yet befall a discreet man to be mistak'n in his choice: and we have plenty of examples. The sobrest and best govern'd men are least practiz'd in these affairs; and who knowes not that the bashfull mutenes of a virgin may oft-times hide all the unlivelines and naturall sloth which is really unfit for conversation; nor is there that freedom of accesse granted or presum'd, as may suffice to a perfect discerning till too late.* [6]

Although Milton's pro-divorce writings caused a stir, and some religious figures reacted with outrage, he also encountered a degree of official support. After Milton presented his argument to the Westminster Assembly, an official committee set up to reform the Church, they recommended that divorce be allowed in cases of abandonment or infidelity. Although this measure was not finally implemented at this stage, it shows that the elite were not fully hostile to the concept of marital breakdown or formalising an existing informal separation.

One example of contemporary concern over this issue is a sermon by Robert Abbot, preached in 1608. During this sermon, he referred to the 'lamentable ruptures and division between husband and wife [that] are everywhere to be seene amongst us'. It seems likely that Robert Abbot felt this was a topic relevant to his congregation and that he came into frequent contact with marital separations. This preoccupation was not limited to individuals. The Church as a whole showed signs of anxiety regarding the extent of marital separations.

This is evident from visitation documents. At Chichester in 1585, local church officials were instructed to discover 'any lawfully married, which offensively live asunder or which have married elsewhere; any man which has two wives or women two husbands'. Similarly, officials were instructed ahead of Cardinal Pole's 1557 visit to Canterbury to investigate 'whether any have put away their wives being not lawfully divorced'.[7]

The repeated raising of this question by church authorities shows that they were concerned about the number of informally separated couples, indicating that marital separations must have occurred fairly frequently from the sixteenth century onwards. Similarly, local censuses covering this time reveal that separation was not unknown, even though it was not the norm. The 1570 Norwich census of the poor revealed that 8.5 per cent of households consisted of deserted wives. One entry describes Margaret Maxwell, a 40-year-old woman whose husband had 'gon from hyr 2 yer' and provided her with 'no comforts'. A census revealed that in 1587, 14 per cent of poor households in Warwick were headed by women abandoned by their husbands.

Sometimes the censuses provide intriguing glimpses into the marriages and personalities of these people; another entry in the 1570 Norwich census describes a 32-year-old man, James Yxford, as an 'evell husbond' to his wife.[8] There is no way of delving further into the lives of James and his wife Susan, but the marriage was obviously not harmonious and the census taker's sympathy clearly lay with Mrs Yxford.

Many men and women who abandoned their marriages went on to marry again. Contemporary reports from 1595 stated that 'unauthorised second marriages were . . . common'. Noted historian Lawrence Stone has referred to bigamy as being a 'flourishing practice of self divorce... amongst the lower and lower middle classes', estimating the practice to run to 'thousands, possibly tens of thousands'.[9] Many factors made it easy for bigamy to take place. Limited means of communication and few travel opportunities allowed people to move away and rid themselves of their past, making it likely that many cases were never discovered. For example, by 1601 a miller named Richard Puncheon had already abandoned two wives, one in Essex and one in Surrey, before proposing to a third lady. His streetwise bride asked him to provide proof that he was a widower as he claimed, so he simply travelled to London where he obtained a forged death certificate. This tactic was also used in 1656 by a Middlesex shoemaker, who forged a banns certificate stating that a couple were free to marry and that their local community had been informed of their impending marriage. In fact, both prospective spouses were already married.[10]

Bigamy was so common that in 1604 Parliament passed an Act making it a crime punishable by death. The passing of this drastic legislation would hardly have been necessary if bigamy had not been a social problem, or if the ecclesiastical courts had proved able to prosecute bigamists successfully. Rather, it was a response to earlier fears that there were no controls against bigamists. Even known cases of bigamy could remain undiscovered if the other spouse was happy to see their partner go. When Robert Tipping and Sarah Roberts married in 1704, Robert was still serving out his apprenticeship to a London upholsterer. Apprentices were not allowed to marry during the course of their apprenticeship, and as such Robert was not able to marry Sarah in a regular church. They therefore became one of the many couples who married clandestinely in the Fleet Prison. The marriage collapsed after ten years, when Robert moved in with his new lover, Elizabeth Hughes and stopped supporting Sarah financially. She sued him twice, for fornication and failing to support her. However, as soon as Robert agreed to settle money on her, she agreed to not bring proof of their marriage to court. Suing him was merely a device intended to force the payment of maintenance.

Sarah only returned to court when Elizabeth Hughes died in 1733, and Robert decided to remarry. Instead of simply doing so, as most people would have done, he sued Sarah for claiming that they had married, insisting that she had only ever been his mistress. By now, Sarah had fallen into dire financial straits. She had been forced to enter the workhouse, was dependent on parish charity, and had been sentenced to six months' hard labour for sheltering her son after he had run away from his apprenticeship, where he was probably badly treated. Robert doubtless assumed that Sarah would not have the will or the financial resources to fight the case, but he had not counted on the support of their (now wealthy) eldest daughter Mary, or his own brother, who testified on Sarah's behalf. Sarah was also able to produce the Fleet Prison's marriage register, as well as her original certificate.

Intriguingly, now that their marriage had been proved valid, Sarah would have been able to apply for further financial support from Robert. However, she did not do so, despite her poverty. The indications are that she considered the marriage had been permanently terminated once she and Robert had agreed on their financial arrangement.[11]

Informal separations were popular with couples of society's lower ranks. They were more geographically mobile as they were not tied to a landed inheritance; they had fewer social obligations; and this was the cheapest separation method available. They were also, however, used by couples further up the social ladder. The most common reason that couples of high social rank chose to separate informally was an issue of honour. Men of high social status were expected to subscribe to a strict patriarchal code which included the responsibility to maintain order within the household, particularly over their wives and children. One example of this was the case of Thomas Elmes and Margaret Verney in 1617. Elmes was quite willing to separate, his only stipulation being that it should be 'done in a way that nobody may know, certainly guess they will but know they need not'. Similarly, in 1686, Sir John Reresby wrote that he would 'suffer in some degree the insolency of a woman rather than make it public to the prejudice of his children'.[12] Ironically, patriarchy could, on occasion, actually work against men, by preventing them from seeking a full separation. Women could exploit this and exercise power by manipulating their husband's wish to keep the separation private.

This happened during the disintegrating marriage of Lady Anne Clifford and the Earl of Dorset in the early seventeenth century. Although the Earl wanted a separation, he was not willing to enter into a formal agreement. Instead, he ordered his servants to leave Lady Anne alone in a house without any means of transportation. Lady Anne, who did not wish for a separation, refused to take the hint and kept following the Earl until he sent word that he no longer wished her to live in his family's homes.[13] In the event, the Earl's reluctance to make their separation public meant that they never had the full separation he wanted, and Lady Anne was able to maintain the semblance of a marriage. Not only could patriarchal behavioural codes be used against men but there was also scope for intelligent women to manipulate these codes against men in order to achieve their aims.

Despite this anxiety regarding the extent of marital breakdown, official attitudes were more lax than might have been expected. Officially, people could report married couples who were living apart, either by themselves or with others, to the Church Courts (commonly known as Bawdy Courts) who would then force the couple to resume cohabitation. In practice, however, people were reluctant to interfere in their neighbours' married lives. As prosecutions were 'dependent on the diligence of communities and local officials in rooting them out',[14] they were likely to fail.

Most courts did not encounter large numbers of separated couples. In Stratford, the Bawdy Court only dealt with six cases concerning marriage throughout the entire sixteenth and seventeenth centuries.[15] Numbers were equally low in Banbury. This gives the impression that married couples did not separate, but in other areas of the country prosecutions were high. In Sussex, for example, 32 couples were presented for living apart, over a period of just seven years.[16] It seems exceedingly unlikely that there was such a dramatic and complete contrast between Stratford and Sussex during the same period. It is more likely that lower ranking church officials were not interested in prosecuting married couples who were separated, and that cases were ignored. In Sussex, even the church officials themselves were occasionally presented for separation, such as 'our curate, Mr Thimble, for living from his wife'. The presence of marital separation even amongst ecclesiastical officials, who were required to maintain a virtuous image, indicates that separation was not necessarily a social taboo. Furthermore, if officials had infringed the rules themselves, it makes it extremely improbable that they would be eager to report unauthorised separations within the parish.

Even when cases were discovered, they were rarely prosecuted. Out of 48 cases in Yorkshire, Cheshire, Suffolk and Somerset, only 2 per cent were actually prosecuted and these were usually targeted because of special circumstances. For example, Richard Mooer, who was cited during Easter 1621 in Sussex, was described as 'a stranger'. This would have made people more wary of him and more inclined to report him as a potential threat to the moral welfare of the village. On other occasions, prosecution notes often referred to extenuating circumstances, suggesting that courts could be lenient towards separated couples. In 1623 John and Ellen Brookes were mentioned:

> *for keeping house apart, by reason that theire children… cannot well agree, making debate betweene them; there for a more quiet and contented living keeps to severall houses, and comes and goes one to another when they think well. Therefore we commit it to your worship's consideration with as much favour as you may too thinke of it.*[17]

The final sentence, with its reference to 'favour', indicates that the local authorities were expected to overlook their separation and take no further action. Even when couples were convicted, punishment was not necessarily forthcoming. No one cited for illicit separation or remarriage in Sussex actually attended the court when called, making it impossible for them to be punished. One of the most glaring examples of the Church Courts' ineffectiveness is that of Richard Hale, who bigamously remarried in Sussex in 1625. After being repeatedly presented, the exasperated court officials wrote to their superiors:

> *we certify unto you that Richard Hale the younger is still remarrying in our parish and stands excommunicated. And we have presented him in every bill and we doe now present him for an excommunicated person, and know not what course to take; therefore we pray you take a course with him.*[18]

Clearly, if Hale cared so little for being excommunicated – the most drastic punishment that a court could impose – there was little else that could be done to censure him. Similarly, the one Stratford bigamist prosecuted 'for marrying two wives' was cited numerous times before he eventually appeared before court, only to disappear before his punishment was pronounced.

Parishioners reporting moral crimes among their neighbours were not overly concerned with separated couples. Church Court records across the country reveal that they were mostly preoccupied with eliminating illegitimacy. Illegitimate children could become a charge upon the parish, as they were dependent on one, instead of two parents, to support them financially. All parish members had a vested interest in preventing this from happening, as it would keep poor rates (and thus their taxes) lower. Separated couples, where both spouses were financially independent, were far less likely to be a charge on the parish, and thus of little interest to the parishioners, or the Church Courts.

The ecclesiastical court system became even more inefficient after the Civil War. There was a 20-year period in which the ecclesiastical courts did not operate, owing to the conflict and their subsequent abolition by the Puritan regime. When they were restored, few were willing to tolerate an intrusion into their private lives which they were no longer used to. After 1660, the Church Courts became increasingly obsolete, confining themselves to prosecuting matters of tax and church attendance until 1720, when they 'virtually collapsed' and faded into insignificance.

This laxness in prosecutions for marital separation and bigamy extended to the secular authorities. One reason why it was easy to escape punishment was the ambiguous nature of the legislation itself. The 1604 Act was explicit and unequivocal in its banning of remarriage, but it was not clear about who precisely was banned from remarrying. While subsequent marriages were declared illegal, those who had engaged in them were not penalised if their spouse had been absent for more than seven years, or if they had previously been separated legally. The Act was badly written and the definitions of whom it intended to punish and under what conditions are not clear.

Even the clergy and judges at the time remained unsure of what the Act was truly intended to enforce. William Whately was one of many Puritan ministers who openly stated that it was perfectly legal and binding to remarry after being separated in an ecclesiastical court. Also, in 1636 Ann Porter was allowed to go free after her lawyers successfully argued that she was exempt from the Act, having been legally separated and even if she was not, 'an ignorant woman'[19] could not be expected to understand the Act. Not only did the judges agree with this, but they advised her to seek a pardon from the King in order to guarantee her safety. This friendly advice indicates that the judges must have had a degree of sympathy towards Ann and her situation, and tells us a great deal about the common attitudes of the day.

There are other examples of lax official attitudes towards bigamy, and even cases of officials accepting the existence of multiple spouses. Katherine Willoughby remarried twice while her first husband was still alive, then in 1607 proceeded to sue both of her husbands at the same time for breaching the dowry agreements they had made.[20] The fact that the Master of Requests allowed her to proceed with this state of affairs, not even remarking upon it, indicates that this was not only a common occurrence, but that the higher orders in society were fairly accepting of this. Many bigamists described their spouses as their 'former' husband or wife, indicating that many people believed that an informal separation had adequately terminated the marriage.

Furthermore, the slack attitude of the courts towards bigamy prosecutions made it an ineffective deterrent to those considering illegal remarriage. Even after the 1604 Act was passed, prescribing the death penalty for bigamists, we can still see indications that the courts on occasion adopted a lax approach to bigamy prosecutions. Spouses were allowed to assume that their husband/wife was dead if they had not seen them in seven years. Most bigamists used this defence, and were treated with according clemency, demonstrating how easy it was to simply deny knowledge that their previous spouse was alive and well.

One of the few who was not treated with such clemency was John Cook, prosecuted for bigamy at the Old Bailey in August 1727. He used the customary defence of claiming 'that he thought his first Wife was dead', but this was not accepted by the judge. This was probably partly due to the fact that he had only been separated for four years, rather than seven, but it was largely a result of witness testimony that he had frequently engaged in 'inhumane Actions and unnatural Expressions' towards his wife when they had cohabited. Witnesses reported that he was 'not allowing her the common Necessaries of Life, and inhumanly turning her out nine Days after her Lying-in [giving birth], saying, if she would not turn out and get to Work he would set the Bed on Fire and cut her Throat'.[21] The court did not look kindly upon these 'inhumane Actions and unnatural Expressions' and sentenced Cook to be branded.

Usually, however, discovery and prosecution did not necessarily lead to punishment. Witnesses and/or certain proof were needed in order to convict a person of bigamy but these were not always forthcoming. One woman was presented for bigamy at the Old Bailey in 1674, yet was acquitted as no witnesses could be found to testify against her.[22] Even if people were found guilty, they could escape death by pleading benefit of clergy. This meant that if the accused could read a passage from the Bible, they were then permitted to receive a lesser punishment, which in the case of bigamy would be branding. Some ingenious people were able to take advantage of this privilege despite being illiterate, by memorising the set passage from the Bible given by the court and pretending to read it.

Only six people were executed for bigamy between the start of records in 1674, and 1800.[23] One was Richard Hazlegrove in July 1677. When he was convicted Hazlegrove attempted to plead benefit of clergy, but it was a desperate move because when the Bible was brought to him, he was unable to read the passage and was consequently sentenced to death. The court scribe wrote beneath this verdict in the official records that it was 'a Case that seems a little severe... which may admonish Parents to bestow, and Children to study at least to read well, since sometimes a man loses his life meerly

31

for want of it'.[24] This personal observation comes close to expressing incredulity at such a severe verdict, hinting that society viewed bigamists with far more tolerance than the laws would indicate.

Although the greater social anonymity of the lower classes made it easier for them to commit bigamy without official retribution, it was by no means absent in the higher ranks. It was, however, a lot more likely that they would be caught. One prominent example was the daughter of the Bishop of Coventry and Lichfield, who married again after she was separated in the ecclesiastical court. Another was Sir Edward Waldegrave, who had married one day, only for his wife to be abducted the next and married to another man, leading to some confusion as to whom she was actually married. The Earl of Devonshire, who married his mistress Penelope Rich in 1605, also had a credible case. They were married in church by a future Archbishop of Canterbury, and Lady Rich had undergone an official separation, but her previous marriage was still considered valid. The continuing uncertainty regarding their legal status juxtaposed with the fact that they attempted to remarry in the first place, suggests that there was a degree of uncertainty about the bounds of what was officially accepted. If the then monarch, James I, had not been set strongly against the philandering couple, it is likely that they would have been fully accepted as husband and wife.

Another notorious bigamous liaison involved Elizabeth, Duchess of Kingston, who was tried for bigamy in 1776. Appointed as Maid of Honour to the Princess of Wales in 1743, she was publicly lauded for her beauty at the time of her secret marriage to Augustus Hervey in 1744. There were many potential advantages to this match, but there were also severe financial drawbacks. Hervey had a good chance of becoming the next Earl of Bristol, and a promising career in the navy, but he was then surviving on an allowance of only £50 a year and his share of prize money from captured enemy ships. Elizabeth would bring no money to the marriage and there was a high probability that Hervey's relatives would not approve. Furthermore, if the marriage was revealed, Elizabeth would have to give up her position as Maid of Honour, which brought her an income of £200 a year. Faced with these obstacles, the couple decided to marry in secret. A few days afterwards, Hervey left for the West Indies, and the couple did not see each other for two years.

Elizabeth must have started to regret the marriage by the time that Hervey returned to England, because it took her two months to meet her husband after his return. They spent a few nights together but Elizabeth used most of this time to convince Hervey to pay her debts. Hervey had also heard disquieting rumours about Elizabeth's flirtations with other men, such as the Duke of Hamilton. The later public admiration of George II led people to whisper that the King intended to make her his mistress. When Hervey returned to sea Elizabeth was pregnant, but the child, a son, died soon after birth. The couple do not appear to have met for many years afterwards.

In 1753, Elizabeth started a serious relationship with the Duke of Kingston. There was no written record of the marriage and at this point it must have seemed easier to pretend the ceremony had never occurred. But she didn't. In 1759, 15 years after the marriage, she visited the vicar who had married them, a Mr Amis, and asked that he make a written declaration of their marriage. As the then Earl of Bristol's health was failing, Hervey's succession to both title and fortune seemed imminent, and Elizabeth was so eager to ensure that the record would be considered valid that she had a lawyer brought to the vicarage to draft the document, and 'concealed herself in a closet' to listen to his advice.

Rumours of Elizabeth's marriage to Augustus Hervey had been circulating for some time. One legal document even referred to her as 'Elizabeth Hervey but commonly called Elizabeth Chudleigh'. In 1767, 23 years after their marriage, Hervey started making plans for a divorce, sending a message to Elizabeth that he had 'the most ample and abundant proofs' of her adultery but that he still wished to 'act on the line of a man of honour', which infuriated Elizabeth. Her biographer, Claire Gervat, believes that this was because she had 'come to believe that the long ago ceremony she had gone through was not a marriage at all'.[25]

Eight years earlier, however, she had gained solid proof of their marriage. It seems more likely that the Duke of Kingston was now willing to marry Elizabeth, but would refuse to marry a scandalous woman who had been convicted of adultery by Parliament. Elizabeth immediately sent back a message saying that she wished Hervey 'to understand that she did not acknowledge him for her legal husband, and should put him to the defiance of such proof'. This made Hervey reconsider his stance, and he took no further steps to divorce Elizabeth.

In 1768, Elizabeth sued for a 'jacitation of marriage' in the ecclesiastical courts. This suit asked the court to declare that there had never been a marriage between Augustus Hervey and herself and that correspondingly, she was a spinster. Hervey countersued, asking the court to declare the opposite. Elizabeth was assisted in her cause by the fact that the vicar, and almost all of the witnesses to the marriage were dead, except a maid named Ann Craddock. Hervey also aided matters by agreeing to not provide 'other proofs of connections or cohabitations', ie providing evidence that he and Elizabeth had had a sexual relationship. Elizabeth took an oath swearing that she was not married (she later said that she could do so, because there were so many other inaccuracies mixed in with the truth of their marriage) and Elizabeth was declared a spinster, free to marry whomsoever she wished.

Within a month, Elizabeth had married the Duke of Kingston, and settled down to what seems to have been a fairly happy married life. She must have thought that her marriage was secure. Just after her wedding to the Duke, Elizabeth would smilingly ask the officiating vicar's widow (who knew about her secret marriage): 'Was it not very good natured of the Duke to marry an old maid?' The matter would have probably died there, were it not for quarrels about the Kingston inheritance. Just five years after their marriage, the Duke died, leaving Elizabeth all his personal wealth and the income from his estates for as long as she did not remarry.

This greatly upset the family of his sister, Lady Frances Meadows, who had assumed that the wealth would pass to them, despite the fact that his dislike of the family was so great that her eldest son had been refused admittance into the house. They decided that their best chance of disinheriting Elizabeth was to find proof that her marriage to the Duke had been bigamous and invalid. They were in luck, for Elizabeth had alienated both Ann Craddock and the vicar's widow, who were willing to tell all they knew. The Meadows family filed a complaint in the Court of Chancery to overthrow the will, claiming that Elizabeth's marriage to the Duke was invalid and that she had forced him to change the will through 'threats and menaces'. Elizabeth was petrified and she fled to France in such haste that she did not even pack a change of clothes. The case gripped the public imagination, and soon a fictionalised account of the Duchess's life called *A Trip to Calais* was being performed on stage. When Elizabeth wrote to the playwright to complain, he merely sent the correspondence to a newspaper.

The courts found in Elizabeth's favour as far as the will was concerned, but she still had to face charges of bigamy. There were reports that she would be held in the Tower of London during the trial, and the *Morning Chronicle* poked fun at the Duchess by reporting that 'an apartment in the Tower is fitting up in a very splendid and elegant style fit for the reception of a lady'.[26] Westminster Hall was set up for a very public trial, and there was a mad scramble for tickets. Spectators queued up for hours before the hall officially opened at 8 am to obtain the best seats, and *The Gazeteer and New Daily Advertiser* wrote that spectators had 'seemed to outvie each other in the richness of their dresses and the brilliancy of their ornaments'.[27] Some humour was added to the proceedings when an Upper Gallery floorboard collapsed underneath the weight of the spectators and two unfortunate women fell through. One plummeted through the hole, kicking the elaborate headdress of the woman beneath her and scattering it around the room, then landing with 'a bare bum squatted on a gentleman's head'. The other lady became stuck in the hole, exposing her naked lower half to the highly amused spectators until she could be freed.

These diversions were considerably more entertaining than the trial itself. By the third day the tickets, which had been so coveted before the trial had begun, were now being advertised for sale in newspapers. Ann Craddock's testimony was harmful, but even more damaging was the testimony of the vicar's widow, who produced the marriage record that Elizabeth had ascertained was legal 17 years before. Elizabeth was, unsurprisingly, found guilty, and she was so distraught that she left England, spending the vast majority of her remaining life in Europe.

One of the most interesting cases of eighteenth century bigamy is that of a fairly well-born lady named Teresia Constantia Philips, but known by her nickname, Con. Her early upbringing was comfortable. The daughter of a lieutenant-colonel in the British Army, Con was sent to an exclusive boarding school in Westminster by her godmother, the Duchess of Bolton, where she was trained to be a lady. Her pampered life, however, was shattered when her mother died in 1721, and her father married a former servant shortly after. She was so frequently at odds with her stepmother that she was forced to leave home the same year, at the age of 12, and set up house in London with her younger sister, whom she supported by taking in sewing. It is doubtful whether this was a fate shared by many of her former Westminster classmates and it is not surprising that she very soon ran into debt to the sum of £500. Penniless and extravagant, Con was being pursued by numerous creditors. She searched around desperately for a solution, and the answer, she decided – as did other penniless, highborn young women at the time – was to marry. Unlike her contemporaries, she had no intention of tying herself permanently to one man. Her solution, instead, was to make a career of bigamy.

In the 1720s, a husband became responsible for paying his wife's debts as well as maintaining her upon marriage, even if the debts had been incurred before the marriage took place. Con was, therefore, advised to marry a stranger in a public church ceremony with the required number of witnesses. The marriage was arranged by a Mr Morrill, who informed Con that her best course of action was to pay him 10 guineas, which 'should procure her a man (already married) who should marry her in another name, and the ceremony should be performed before such witnesses as should, when called upon, prove it, and by that means screen her from debt'. This would be enough to absolve her from responsibility for any of her present or future debts.

The groom, however, a man named Delafield, was already married. By marrying a man who was already married, Con was still, in theory, a single woman yet the public nature of the marriage ceremony was enough to keep her creditors from pursuing her for payment. When Delafield appeared two hours late at the church, he was so drunk that he had to be held up at the altar. After he and Con were thrown into bed together in front of witnesses, Delafield disappeared into thin air and Con was, theoretically, both married and free.

After this, Con was at liberty to continue her numerous marriages and love affairs. Two years after her marriage to Delafield, she married a wealthy man named Henry Muilman, who was told by various lawyers that, as Delafield had married Con bigamously, she was free to marry again whenever she wished. Con might have lived peacefully as Muilman's wife, if rumours had not reached his parents about her previous marriage, destroying family relations. Con grew suspicious that Muilman was intending to abandon her, and started to break into cabinets to read his letters. The situation deteriorated until their final encounter, when she asked her father-in-law how she had offended him, and he replied: 'Why, I am told you were a common whore before you married my son'. Predictably, relations came to an end.

Muilman, faced with financial ruin without his father's support, threatened Con to try and force her into lying about the validity of her first marriage, beating her and claiming that he would have her imprisoned in a madhouse. She responded by depositing all her important possessions and her finest clothes, worth more than £1,000, in a bank. Events took a desperate turn when Delafield reappeared and sued Con for adultery in an attempt to extract money from her, and Muilman threw her out of the house. Even after this, though, he still continued to visit her. On one memorable occasion, frustrated by her refusal to let him into her bed, Muilman appeared at her door with a gang of men at 2 am, demanding entrance. She warned the gang that if they did not leave the premises then she would shoot them. When they laughed at her, she filled a pistol with firework powder, and fired at them, making such a great noise that they fled. When Muilman complained to a judge, swearing that Con had tried to murder him, the judges were so amused at the story that they let her go, saluting her as she entered the courtroom.

Unfortunately, her success was short-lived. When Con removed all her belongings from safekeeping, Muilman and his gang intercepted her on the way to the theatre and decked out in her finery, removing between £1,000 and £1,500 of jewels from her and stripping her almost naked. After this, Con was in such dire financial straits that she was forced to accept Muilman's proposed financial settlement of £200 a year, as well as her jewels and plate. However, she made her greatest mistake when she went to Muilman for a loan of £700 to clear her debts. He would only give her the money if she deposited their signed financial agreement with him. When she repaid the money, he refused to return the deed, leaving her with no proof of their agreement and no better off than she had been before.

In later life, she became the mistress of a wealthy heir, whom she never named in her memoirs, meaning she had been twice married, and another man's mistress at only 16 years of age. Several more affairs followed; one with Sir Herbert Pakington, who attempted to stab himself with his sword when she announced her intention of leaving him; another with an anonymous plantation owner, whom she pursued to Boston and Jamaica. Despite several more bigamous marriages, Con spent two years in prison for debt, eventually resorting to blackmailing her lovers and husbands by threatening to publicly reveal details of their relationships. When blackmail did not bring her enough money, she published an account of her life, detailing her various marital and extra-marital exploits. It gained her a considerable amount of publicity but despite her numerous money-making schemes and lovers, she was heavily in debt and alone when she died in 1765.[28]

The dubious nature of Con's various marriages made it unclear which one, if any, should be considered binding. This confused state of affairs continued into later years, when Henry Muilman wished to remarry. He tried initially to seek a formal separation, having his marriage annulled on the grounds that she was already married to Delafield. This needed Con's agreement, and she would easily have been able to prove that her marriage to Delafield was invalid at the time, as he was already married.

A legal and ecclesiastical expert, Dr Paul, advised the father of Muilman's prospective second wife that: 'I would not marry a daughter of mine to Mr Muilman… for to my certain knowledge he is lawfully the husband of Mrs Philips, if you insist upon it I will… grant you a license'. Clearly, a fairly lax attitude towards both marriage and marital separation still existed during the eighteenth century, if experts were willing to infringe the law and grant licences for marriages they believed to be technically invalid. On a personal level, fathers were willing to ignore legalities as long as their daughters would be socially recognised as wealthy, married women. What really mattered in the early modern era was the outward appearance of being single or married, and not the legal truth.

This confused state of affairs led to some peculiar situations. Individuals could manipulate marital separation for their own, sometimes nefarious, means. One distressing example was that of Elizabeth and John Norris in 1641. Elizabeth Norris wrote that she had 'divorced' her husband, Henry Mullon, in an ecclesiastical court 'many years before'. By this she meant that she had obtained a legal separation. After this, unsurprisingly, she did not see Mullon again. Elizabeth took advantage of the rule that spouses were free to remarry after seven years of no contact. She actually took more precautions than other women, only marrying after hearing a 'relation of his death by some of his neere Friends'. She then married a wealthy man, appropriately named Mr Rich, who died two years later, leaving her with a substantial amount of property and children by both of her husbands.

She must have been fairly attached to Mr Rich because she waited seven years to marry a third time, unfortunately choosing the unscrupulous and cunning John Norris. This marriage officially transferred all her property to Norris, yet she tried to make sure that she would retain some legal protection by drawing up a legal deed that would give her both dower rights in the estate and a personal allowance. While John Norris agreed to this, he had a few tricks up his sleeve. At some point, he had discovered that Elizabeth had never found a record of her first husband's death.

When Elizabeth questioned him about his refusal to give her an allowance out of her own fortune, Norris threatened her that if she did not withdraw her financial demands 'he would sue a nullity of the... marriage' on the grounds that it was bigamous, and that Elizabeth was still married to Henry Mullon, who was then still alive. Courageously, being sure that Mullon had indeed died many years before, she refused to give in to Norris's threats and insisted that he fulfil his obligations. He went ahead, however, and at Easter 1636, he had their marriage declared invalid and Elizabeth branded a bigamist. Somehow, despite the fact that their marriage had been annulled, he retained all her property and inheritance from Mr Rich, refusing to give her either her dower rights or the personal allowance they had previously agreed on. Together with her children, Elizabeth was 'deprived of her estate and all legal remedies... opposing her to great misery and the charity of her friends'.

In 1634, she succeeded in having her case heard in Chancery, where she was admitted as a pauper under an early form of legal aid. She asked either for the deed to be enforced and to be regarded as a married woman, or for her late husband's estate to be returned to her. Norris succeeded in delaying the case several times by using tactics such as giving insufficient answers to Elizabeth's allegations, and accusing her and her trustees of 'many nontruths and Scandals'. He told her that he would spend £2,000 (presumably the entire worth of Mr Rich's estate) before he would give her anything. These efforts evidently came to nothing, as two years later Elizabeth was submitting her petition to Parliament, begging them to intercede, describing herself as 'miserable poor, and distressed, and so inept' to do battle with John Norris. Although there was a tendency to hyperbole in this era, and Elizabeth was clearly being supported by trustees, it must have grated upon her that Norris had managed to slip through all legal nets. He had contrived to terminate their marriage and still retain her property, which should, in theory, have been impossible. She was also responsible for supporting the children of all her marriages. Another hand, probably that of Elizabeth Norris, has inserted after the description of her poverty the words 'not withstanding that he hath issue by her'.[29] Parliamentary records are silent on the eventual fate of Elizabeth Norris, but her case does show us the enormous degree of personal variation that existed in the fates of those accused of bigamy and unofficial separation in early modern England. While many escaped the system, there were always opportunities for individuals to manipulate the system maliciously to cause others harm.

It was even easier to abandon a clandestine marriage than a conventional one. As clandestine marriages, such as those performed in the Fleet Prison, were not under official ecclesiastical jurisdiction, ecclesiastical officials could act without regulation within the prison confines, performing legal marriages without any restrictions whatsoever. People could then exploit the resulting difficulty of obtaining evidence to have the marriage declared fictional. If records were taken, which they were not always, they were easier to lose or obtain/forge from unscrupulous keepers. For example, Henry Muilman, one of the many husbands of Con Philips, made several attempts to obtain the original copy of Con Philips's marriage certificate. One particularly ingenious attempt involved him making friends with the landlord of the book's owner, and persuading him to demand the book as rent security. Although Robert Tipping was discovered trying to cover up his marriage after the relationship had collapsed, this was solely due to the fact that his daughter, who had an obvious vested interest in ensuring that her legitimacy was publicly confirmed, had made an exceptionally good marriage. She was now able to provide her mother with the financial support necessary to legally prove the marriage valid. Otherwise, Tipping would easily have been able to erase the marriage officially. This is especially important as those engaging in Fleet marriages would have been likely to have a low socio-economic status, thus making it even more probable that they would not have had the financial resources necessary to construct a defence.

Another example which shows how easy it could be to escape a Fleet marriage was that of Robert Feilding, who married two women at the same time, one of whom was the Duchess of Cleveland, former mistress of Charles II. He became known as a notorious fortune hunter, exceptionally promiscuous even by the standards of the licentious court of Charles II, and exceptionally good-looking. One early issue of *Tatler* from 1709 described him as 'the universal flame of all the fair sex'.

As he was in need of a large injection of money, during the summer of 1705 Feilding courted two women: the Duchess and a widow named Anne Deleau, who had recently been left an exceptionally large fortune of £60,000, the equivalent of nearly £5 million today. Anne Deleau, however, was extremely difficult to find, living a reclusive life and avoiding society. A less determined man would have given up, but Feilding was not willing to give up the possibility of £60,000. He located Anne's hairdresser and bribed her to arrange a meeting with Mrs Deleau. The hairdresser, Mrs Villiers, knew that this would not be possible but, reluctant to give up the promised £500, arranged that a prostitute named Mary Wadsworth should take Anne's place. She must have been a very good actress, as Feilding was completely taken in and, despite 'Anne's' ostensible reluctance, she 'allowed' herself to be persuaded into marriage. Just under a fortnight after this ceremony, he also married the elderly Duchess of Cleveland, and shortly after that, began an affair with her granddaughter Charlotte Calvert (whom we will encounter later), leaving him with two wives and a mistress to keep happy.

This situation continued until May 1706, when Feilding found out that he had been duped by (the now pregnant) Mary Wadsworth. Predictably, he did not react calmly, attacking her in the street. He also attacked the hairdresser, Mrs Villiers, threatening her with a hammer, locking her in a closet, and threatening her that: 'If ever you mention my being married to that bitch my wife, I will have your flesh stripped from your bones, and your bones bruised'.

This was not a wise move. Neither Mrs Villiers nor Mary Wadsworth were easily intimidated. They told their story to the Duke of Grafton, the Duchess of Cleveland's grandson, who in turn told his grandmother. The Duchess, understandably, made a fearful scene; Feilding attacked her and law enforcement forces soon arrived to break the fight up. He was taken to jail but was released shortly afterwards, forcing the Duchess to flee her home in Bond Street with all her goods until she could prove that their marriage had been bigamous.

Feilding was not the sort of person to accept defeat. Upon his release from prison, he placed a newspaper advert, ordering the Duchess to return to her legal husband. The Duchess retaliated by publishing his letters to Mary Wadsworth, which are still fairly explicit by the standards of today. In one letter, Feilding wrote, 'Methinks I fucked you again with the height of pleasures, and fucked and fucked till I dissolved with pleasure'. Although he had been discovered, he was still able to take action to evade prosecution. He immediately constructed a defence, sending the priest who had married him and Mary Wadsworth to work as a missionary in China and bribing a keeper of the Fleet marriage registers to forge an entry of an earlier marriage by Mary Wadsworth.

The Duchess, however, was able to employ some of the best and most diligent lawyers of the time. They searched through every single Fleet marriage register in existence and made notes of the cases two weeks before Feilding bribed the keeper. When the record appeared squeezed on to the bottom of the page, therefore, the Duchess's lawyers had incontrovertible proof that it had been forged. Faced with such evidence, he was convicted but he escaped the death penalty by pleading benefit of clergy, and then avoided being branded by mysteriously obtaining a pardon from Queen Anne. His story ended as bizarrely as it began, with his reconciliation with Mary Wadsworth, to whom he later left his estate.[30] Perhaps he had at last found a woman whom he could respect as his equal.

The lack of legal control over spouses who abandoned their marriages meant that women could, if they were determined, take similar actions to men in initiating and arranging a separation. Although these women are difficult to trace, we have enough sparsely documented examples to demonstrate that it was not unknown. Many historians have assumed that few women would abandon a marriage, as they were in need of financial support while raising a family. This model, however, did not fit all women and monetary pressures were not always a barrier. The increasing number of wars associated with the expansion of the British Empire and the resulting trade opportunities during the eighteenth century meant that women could gain autonomy through the absence of their husbands. Annabelle Bunting (whom we will encounter while exploring parliamentary divorces) eloped while her husband was supervising their estates on the island of St Christopher.

On other occasions, maintenance might be offered to the abandoned wife. In spite of the fact that Henry Muilman transferred his estate to his brother to avoid Con Philips obtaining a portion, and that the marriage was of doubtful legality in the first place, she was still awarded an annual income of £200 and a lump sum payment of £2,000. While financial considerations certainly were a prohibitive issue, this was not true for all women, especially those with resources of their own.

Some women did not have the financial burden of children to support, others were happy to abandon their children, and in some cases their husband had not contributed to their financial upkeep in the first place. These women could and did find ways to support themselves in order to escape an unhappy marriage. Lettice Betts pawned her household goods in order to fund her elopement in 1609.[31] Similarly, Elizabeth Hunt abandoned her children in 1657. She eloped with a schoolmaster, leaving her six children behind and forcing her husband, Thomas, to put an advertisement in the newspaper appealing for any information regarding her whereabouts. It is unlikely that he felt too downhearted about her disappearance; the advertisement described Elizabeth as fat, shrivelled and with rotten teeth, in contrast to her young lover. He was more distressed by the disappearance of the goods she had taken with her which were worth £200.[32] Not all of these women were naïve or easily deceived. Woe betide the man who attempted to betray Ellen Goulsborough, who threatened her lover in 1621 that she would 'cut his throat or poison him' if he double crossed her.[33] Not all women were passive victims.

One woman who did not have a happy ending to her marital separation was Alice Millikin, who migrated to London with her son David, to work as a cleaner and nurse in the late seventeenth century.

Originally from Herefordshire, she had worked together with her husband as a glove maker but he had grown indifferent to both his family and his work, leaving Alice as the family's sole breadwinner. 'After a considerable waiting for his Amendment', she took her children and went to London, presumably in the hope that she would find more work. Initially she did but after losing her job, poverty, together with an acquaintance named Mrs Chaston, led her into 'coin clipping', an early form of counterfeiting. This method involved shaving off parts of coins, which were then made into new coins. Alice seems to have been on the fringes of the operation. She knew that there was a gang of operatives but she denied ever meeting them, saying that her only point of contact was Mrs Chaston. Despite this, she was sentenced to be executed by burning at the stake, the usual punishment for seventeenth century counterfeiters. Even the officials felt sorry for her and 'endeavour'd to comfort her, for she seemed very penitent', before leaving her to her grisly fate.[34]

Women could play an exceptionally active role in arranging their own separations within breakaway religious groups. Nowadays, we tend to assume (with the exception of the Reformation) that the majority followed the state religion and had the same religious beliefs. In fact, this was not necessarily the case. During the English Civil War, tensions between the Church of England and Puritans, as well as the breakdown of religious discipline, allowed different religious groups to emerge, such as Baptists, Quakers, Ranters and Muggletonians. These groups held what were considered radical views, not least about the role that women should play in society. For example, most of these groups believed that women should play an instrumental role in preaching and guiding interpretations of the Bible, at a time when women were expected to take direction from male priests fond of citing St Paul's instruction to women 'to keep silence in the congregation'.

Another belief these groups held was that people could dissolve their marriages at will, especially if their spouses did not share their extreme religious views. It was reported that women belonging to radical sects were fond of chants such as, 'We will not be wives, And tie up our lives, To villainous slavery'. The most notorious militant woman who cast off her husband was a female sectarian preacher named Mrs Attoway. After giving a sermon, she started to discuss her thoughts on divorce with members of her congregation, ending by saying that 'she for her part would look more into it, for she had an unsanctified husband, that did not walk in the way of Sion, nor speak the language of Canaan'.[35]

After the group expressed their approval, she not only separated from her husband but remarried a fellow sectarian named William Jenney, who had earlier separated from his wife on the same religious grounds. Although the number of these cases were probably overstated by enemies who were afraid that these religious sects would take over, and were trying to paint a picture of a lawless society, there are enough named cases to suggest that unofficial divorces did occur within these groups. Most of these religious groups were short-lived, yet during their lifetime they gave women the power to dissolve their previous marriages and build new lives with alternative partners.

Although reactions to separated women varied depending on the circumstances and the individuals involved, society was not, by and large, hostile to them. Women could and did request help in separating from their husbands from either family members or neighbours. This valuable assistance was often provided by other women, and could extend across class boundaries. Margaret Jones, a mid-sixteenth century widow, had evidently grown close to her maid Judith, as she attended Judith's wedding when she married and left the Jones household. They remained in contact, for Margaret gave Judith and her husband marriage counselling when the marriage first developed problems. Afterwards, when Judith's marriage turned physically abusive, Margaret provided Judith with a home and testified on her behalf during the subsequent legal proceedings.[36]

Women also played an influential role as makers and breakers of reputation and 'credit', a particularly important matter in early modern society. Local news and opinions were largely spread through female gossip networks, and women's judgement played a prominent role in determining the local community's view of the separation.

Unsurprisingly, they were usually on the side of the wife, and men worried about their power. Robert Burnam attributed his financial ruin to his estranged wife, Elizabeth. He accused her of scattering leaflets around town libelling him and using the gossip networks to spread untruths about him. This apparently ruined his reputation and livelihood, as afterwards no one would approach his business.[37] In 1699, George Parker told a similar story. His business rival took great pleasure in publicising his wife's claims that he had seduced their maid, while beating her and imprisoning her, thus destroying his business.

One ingenious and horrific way in which men could separate from their wives was by imprisoning them in an asylum. The eighteenth century saw a rise of complaints in the law courts that men were imprisoning their wives in private asylums. Historian Elizabeth Foyster has convincingly argued that as wife beating increasingly became seen as unacceptable, men instead started to punish their wives by constraining them. Although it began simply as a punishment, some men found that it was more convenient to lock their wives up permanently, abandoning them in an asylum.

The growth of private madhouses in the eighteenth century made this an increasingly viable option for husbands. There were around 50 licensed madhouses in England by 1800, but there were probably many more unlicensed institutions. Having someone committed was not difficult. Private asylums in the eighteenth century were run on a profitable basis, giving owners an incentive not to ask too many questions when a husband declared that his wife needed to be locked away for her own good. There was room for manipulation even when a wife was genuinely mentally troubled. Alice Shepheard was sent to an asylum in 1770 after marital problems led to her being judged mentally ill. By 1775 she was deemed to be fully cured but Alice's husband deliberately refused to pay Alice's board fees so that she would continue to be imprisoned. A family friend declared that Alice's husband intended 'to have her kept where she is now in hopes it will shorten her days'.[38]

There were no asylum regulations at all before 1774, giving the owners free reign over their admittance procedures. Regulation was finally implemented after an alarming House of Commons report in 1763, which described a madhouse in Chelsea where on inspection, none of the married women there were found to be insane. One employee admitted that during the course of his six-year employment there, he had never dealt with a genuine lunatic.

The 1774 Act For Regulating Private Madhouses required, amongst other regulations, for a doctor to certify that a patient was genuinely insane. This still would not have helped one of the wives imprisoned, Hannah McKenzie, whose husband had had her locked up in 1766. She had brought up several nieces but later found that her husband, Peter, was having an affair with one of them. When she confronted him, he did not attempt to deny it. He instead announced that her niece should take over Hannah's role as mistress of the Harley Street household, and that Hannah was no longer entitled to give orders to the servants or to use the family carriage. Hannah's fortune was largely supporting the McKenzie household and she was not willing to give up her authority. Peter started to invite doctors specialising in insanity to visit the household. Hannah fled but Peter tricked her into returning, and upon her return, imprisoned her in her room under the care of a psychiatric nurse. She was placed in a straitjacket and the windows were screwed shut in order to prevent her from drawing attention to herself. She tried to escape, but was instead taken to a madhouse in Paddington, where she eventually managed to make contact with a gardener working in the house next door by throwing down her shoe. The asylum had clearly not searched Hannah thoroughly because she had enough money to throw down to the boy as a bribe. By doing so, she managed to get word to her friends of her whereabouts, so that they could organise her release.

Hannah's case illustrated that even when medical professionals were involved, either self-interest or incompetence could render their presence useless in protecting an innocent wife. It is also worth bearing in mind that in order to free a woman from a madhouse, someone outside the institution had to provide evidence of the woman's sanity to a Judge of the King's Bench for him to issue a writ of *Habeas*

Corpus, requiring the jailor to produce the lady in court. If Hannah had not been able to get a message to her friends, it is very likely that she would have stayed there. Yet, people seem to have been willing to help falsely imprisoned women; in 1759 it was reported that more than 3,000 people protested in Bethnal Green when a husband had wrongly committed his wife to a madhouse but this was dependent on knowledge of a wife's imprisonment ever reaching the outside world.[39]

Official attempts to force couples to reconcile were frequently doomed to failure. Ecclesiastical courts proved inefficient and ineffective even at the height of their influence, and lost virtually all their power to intervene in marital disputes after their abolition and restoration in the 1660s. Secular courts faced many problems in prosecuting bigamists. Uncertainty as to whom the legislation applied to prevented effective prosecution, while many were reluctant to turn people in to the courts, as the penalty for bigamous remarriage was harsh and unjustified. People met with mixed fates as a result of their marriage breakdown. Some husbands and wives escaped relatively unscathed from their marital troubles, ready to start the journey to a happier life. The Duchess of Kingston had her marriage declared invalid, but she was still able to live a life of relative ease and luxury on the Continent with the inherited wealth from her supposed husband. Other spouses, such as the condemned Alice Milikin, met with penury and death. From imprisoning a wife in an asylum to forging certificates to commit bigamy, marital separation was rarely a mundane affair!

CHAPTER 3

Legal Battles:
Tricking the Law

In the mid-seventeenth century, the Widow Blackacre, a character in William Wycherley's play *The Plain Dealer*, told a packed theatre that marriage for a woman was 'worse than excommunication in depriving her of the benefit of the law'.[40] Until the late Victorian era, marriage deprived a woman of many legal rights that were available to both widows and single women. Not only was her property considered to belong to her spouse, but a vengeful husband could sue people for providing his runaway wife with financial or practical assistance. Living apart from a husband could be hazardous for a woman. Legal practice, however, did not always follow legal theory, especially in the 1500s and 1600s. There were wives who sued their husbands through courts in order to obtain a regular allowance, or the return of their goods or land. Another form of legal separation could be issued through an ecclesiastical court, where a spouse could sue for a separation 'from bed and board', regardless of the other partner's wishes. This provided women with a degree of security, although, as we shall see, they were not always successful.

Historian Martin Ingram has argued that cases of formal separation were 'evidently very uncommon', citing the small number of recorded cases that can be found today.[41] However, it is worth bearing in mind that many crucial marital separation documents have simply not survived. Many formal separation cases also were never recorded. Records cannot tell us about informal agreements between husband and wife that were never brought to court, either because they were adhered to or because disputes were resolved by other means. This would indicate that although the actual number of cases is low, they could just be a small fraction of the separations that took place in England from the Tudors to the Victorians.

There has been a great deal of debate as to how easy official separations were to obtain from courts. Some historians have classified the ecclesiastical courts as ineffective for a wife wishing to separate from her husband, as they were more focused on persuading the couples to reunite. Some women found themselves totally abandoned by the courts. In 1532/3, a wife named Edith Mathew sued for separation in the ecclesiastical courts, describing how her marriage had turned violent and miserable after the couple had begun quarrelling over her husband's children by a previous marriage. She came before Archbishop Warham, the Archbishop of Canterbury and the most senior personages in the pre-Reformation Church. He was unsympathetic to her case and ordered Edith to reconcile with her husband.

Some women, however, sued successfully for a legal separation. Anne Disbrow sued her husband, first for assault in the civil courts, and subsequently for separation in the ecclesiastical courts in 1672.[42] Her two-year marriage had been marred by an ongoing legal battle between her parents and her in-laws, who were quarrelling over her dowry. The final straw came when Anne was severely beaten after she refused to sleep with her husband one night, and appeared before the Mayor of Cambridge bruised, battered and spitting blood. The civil court dismissed the charges of assault and battery. They seem to have felt that her sexual refusal and the legal dispute had justly provoked her husband. Her refusal to sleep with her husband was seen as refusing him his marital rights, and her support of her parents seen as a betrayal of her husband and his family. The ecclesiastical court, however, must have had some sympathy, for it granted her a separation, along with maintenance payments until one of their deaths.

This hit-and-miss approach may be one reason why we see couples increasingly bypassing the ecclesiastical courts and resorting to the civil courts in an attempt to gain financial provision. If a wife had the necessary resources to obtain a legal separation, then the courts could offer her a degree of protection. Despite coverture rules giving husbands control over their wife's possessions, surviving cases show that some women were given autonomy over the property that they brought into the marriage. In one early example from the 1530s, Elizabeth, Lady Butler, is ceded control over lands and tenements inherited from her former husband 'as though no such marriage between them had be[en] made and solemnized'.[43]

There were also methods to force an erring husband to pay maintenance for the support of his wife. Court records contain a number of examples of separated wives of all social classes taking their husbands to court to provide them with maintenance. One of these women was Dame Margery Acton in 1553. The court agreed and 'ordered and decreed that the said Sir Robert [Acton] shall from henceforth yearly content and pay to the said Dame Margery [Acton] the sum of £30 of English money yearly during his life'.[44]

They could also be accompanied by an early form of restraining order. Alice Bellnappe from Warwickshire did not limit herself to asking that she be appointed a percentage of her husband's profits as 'shall be thought mete and convenient' but requested too that she be given the money 'without any meddling therein to be had', and that her husband was 'never to resort nor come unto the company'of Alice and her family.[45] Joan Spragin also obtained an order from an ecclesiastical court that specifically freed her from any 'disturbance' from her husband.

There were also legal resources for women who required financial support. Litigation could be expensive. It required travel to London, then the payment of legal fees and accommodation while the litigants stayed in London. The Court of Requests provided a way for poorer litigants to sue as cheaply as possible. Isabell Osmoderley used this court in 1555. Twenty years before, when she married William Osmoderley, her father granted him lands valued at £40. Since then, the marriage had broken down and William was using violence to keep Isabell out of the house and refusing her any money or property, even out of the lands allocated for her own personal use. This eventually forced her to journey from Cumberland to London where she could rely on the 'aid and help of her friends'.[46]

Assistance could even come in an early form of legal aid. When Griffith Jones submitted a complaint against his wife Marion and her associates, he declared that he was a poor man who could not afford to sue her. Having satisfied the court that this was the case, the judge wrote that Jones should be provided with free legal assistance from a court-appointed lawyer. Similarly, Joan Spragin was admitted '*in forma pauperis*', allowing her to sue her husband without legal expenses.

The support of a wife's community was also of great significance. The importance of 'friends' in influencing a woman's actions should not be underestimated. Friends could greatly facilitate a woman's ability to leave her husband, while a lack of support would restrain her. Some neighbours were willing to provide temporary financial support while the case proceeded through the courts. Margaret Littleton was sustained on 'my neighbours' charitable devotion both in diet and lodging'.[47] Isabell Osmoderley was at pains to stress that she had only involved the court as her husband 'would never here unto assent there unto' contact with her representatives.[48] This indicates that the court would normally have expected separations to be worked out between the couple and their friends and family.

Dame Margery Acton's plea to the Court of Requests in 1553 reveals that the support of one's friends was vital for survival as a separated wife in the sixteenth century. While her friends had previously been willing to support her, they eventually decided that 'she hath been and is such a burden to all her friends as they are now waxed utterly weary of her and will trust her no more'.[49] Dependence was clearly not always a sustainable option.

There were laws prohibiting people from aiding, abetting and/or preventing a runaway wife to live apart from her husband. Some historians, such as Lawrence Stone, have pointed to this law as conclusively preventing women from rebuilding their lives, either with a new, informal partner or from living with another family member or friend for company and protection. While this was the formal letter of the law, however, there are indications that this was not as strictly applied in practice as would be expected. For example, in 1799 Robert

Wheeler was acquitted by the King's Bench of assisting his daughter to separate from her husband, saying that his home was the 'natural and most proper place' for her to go since she was 'compelled to leave her husband's home by reason of cruel treatment'.[50]

There are also documents demonstrating that women could, on occasion, play an active role in hindering marital separations. One especially interesting case is the marital breakdown of Elizabeth and William Walter. In 1641, a parliamentary committee had ostensibly ordered the couple to reconcile, but then immediately afterward made financial provision for Elizabeth in the event that this reconciliation failed to materialise. Even the committee seems to have had their doubts about their ability to reunite a warring couple.

In 1646, amongst the administrative and legal chaos of the Civil War, William Walter appealed to Parliament for a legal separation on the grounds that Elizabeth had cheated on him. She successfully counter appealed, stating that:

> she is not guilty of any such fault... of her husband's disloyalty to her bed and that it is already publicly known that for the space of five years... her said husband kept a maid servant in his house while [she] lived with him by whom he had two illegitimate children and forbore your petitioner's company for all the said times and suffered your petitioner to provide for the said Children as for his own children lawfully begotten.[51]

This case demonstrates two main points. Firstly, that Parliament was willing to hear and give credence to the wife's side of the case, and secondly, that women possessed enough knowledge of patriarchal ideology to argue their case skilfully in a way that would demonstrate that errant husbands were unable or unwilling to fulfil their patriarchal responsibilities. For example, Elizabeth Walter largely bases her defence on her husband's adultery. While to a certain extent a sexual double standard did exist, people's acceptance of this hinged on specific rules. One of these rules was that adultery should be kept as private as possible. Another was that the adultery could not affect the domestic life of the wife. Elizabeth Walter's petition has clearly been written in such a manner as to highlight the different ways in which her husband has not fulfilled his patriarchal obligations, such as prioritising his mistress and their children over his legitimate family. She obviously expected that Parliament would agree that his refusal to follow these rules meant that he had abdicated the right to superiority over his wife, thus losing the ability to engage in adultery without censure. We can see that this was successful by the fact that the divorce bill failed to pass the Commons. By refusing to follow the strictures of patriarchy, William Walter had forfeited his petition for divorce.

Although men seemingly acted from a position of unrestrained power, it is clear that many men were constrained by their patriarchal duties and wished to maintain a reputation and good 'credit' with their neighbours. Men who did not fulfil these responsibilities laid themselves open to disapproval. In the 1550s, Elizabeth Bourne wrote to her husband Anthony, 'I wonder that you [have gone] against your credit to break it concerning you have several deeds under your own land and seal and persons of good credit to witness against you'. Anthony Bourne's reluctance to live up to his patriarchal responsibilities was so great that Elizabeth Bourne's relatives sanctioned their separation on those grounds. Furthermore, Elizabeth drew a great distinction between the actions of her husband, and of those men who were supporting him, writing, 'They know not, Mr Bourne, how little profit you tooke... [your] Desertion of dissident life, by imprisonment, nor have many misbegotten bastards... by Mrs Paynam and others, nor have you increased them by many sundrie women'.[52]

Her drawing of this distinction indicates that Elizabeth Bourne was implying that if her husband's supporters knew of his sexual misdemeanours, they would immediately cease to support him. There is, therefore, a hint of blackmail. This demonstrates how women could use gender norms and patriarchal ideology to secure the upper hand in separation negotiations.

In some marital separation cases, such as that of Marion and Griffith Jones, wives were the sole breadwinners in the household and were consequently ordered to pay their husband's maintenance. On 11

February 1594, Griffith Jones, a skinner, submitted a complaint to the court against, not only his wife, 70-year-old Marion Jones, but nine of her neighbours. He alleged that Marion had been effectively brainwashed by her neighbours to 'swear the peace' against him and withhold his household goods, such as furniture.

'Swearing the peace' meant taking an oath that there was a strong likelihood that another individual would attempt to harm you. If a magistrate could be convinced that there were good reasons behind these fears, they would bind the aggressor over to keep the peace, forcing them to find someone to act as a financial guarantor that no violent acts would be committed. If they could not find a guarantor, then they would be imprisoned. It was, therefore, a serious accusation. Even though Griffith Jones had tried to solve matters amicably, through mediators appointed by the Mayor of London, his wife had refused to accept any conditions.

The neighbours Griffith had accused responded through their own petition, refuting all of his allegations. Instead, they described him as 'a man given much... to trouble and contention', who had married Marion, a widow with money and inheritance of her own, to 'lie at his ease' while she supported him. They seem to have been correct. In 1577, he had been whipped to punish him for his incontinent living, and on another occasion his parish income was stopped due to his numerous arguments with his son. Most tellingly, when he was awarded a pension, it was given on the condition that he did not sue people without just cause.

The Jones's neighbours attributed the marriage breakdown to a quarrel over housing. Griffith wished to sell their current house, which Marion had inherited from her first husband, and she refused to leave. Infuriated at her refusal to agree, Griffith started to beat and abuse his wife, and when even this did not produce the desired effect, he abandoned her to live in lodgings. While the local parson did attempt to intervene in an early form of marital counselling, it was to no avail.

Meanwhile, Griffith received maintenance out of Marion's earnings, of three shillings and four pence each week. Not satisfied with this, however, Griffith hatched a plot with a friend, Rhys Jones, to obtain the household goods and furniture that had been left behind when he abandoned Marion. In court, he pretended that Rhys Jones had loaned him money but he now did not have the resources to repay him. Consequently, the bailiffs were sent to Marion's house and, as the couple were still married, were able to take goods from her house considered equal in value to the amount of the supposed debt.

The neighbourhood apparently rose up against the plot. A mob gathered outside Marion's house when the bailiffs arrived, and started a two-pronged attack, removing the goods and harassing the officials so brutally that they said they 'would not take the like office in hand to do again for 20 nobles' (around £1,000 today). Objects were removed from the house, then thrown over the wall connecting Marion's house with that of a neighbour, who in turn, passed the objects to the house next door. Frustrated by the lack of official response, the neighbourhood had clearly chosen to take matters into their own hands.

The plot destroyed a lifetime's worth of hard work (Marion was over 70 years old at this time) and it left her impoverished. Enraged by this deception, Marion's friends and neighbours took it upon themselves to try and resolve the situation. Firstly they tried to convince Rhys to have 'some remorse and pity' for her and allow her to retain some of her goods. When this did not work, they petitioned the Lord Mayor of London on behalf of Marion to intervene in the case. When the Mayor refused to do so, one of her neighbours, John Rowdon, paid the bailiff more than £12 to buy some of the goods back. Their disgust at Griffith Jones's actions has survived over the years, thanks to the record of their answer to the court. In a rare diversion from the legal procedures and forms, the defendants state in a somewhat annoyed tone that 'if the said complainant cannot be relieved with any part or parcel of his own goods, but is driven to great extremity and need, he may thank himself thereof by reason of his said practice... with the said Rhys Jones'. Griffith had clearly made himself extremely unpopular with the local community, and there seems to have been a strong belief that he was intentionally defrauding Marion.[53]

After the neighbours cast aspersions on his character, Griffith's claims took a more menacing tone. He begins to describe Marion as 'evil', a 'wicked woman' and a 'serpent'. His complaint shifts its focus to violence, claiming that she had started to hide knives in their bed in order to kill him in his sleep; a bizarre allegation to introduce so late in the process. He also claims that he had been cornered by groups of the neighbourhood women who would verbally abuse him. This particular allegation was probably a result of him physically abusing Marion. Griffith had punched his wife in the face, making her bleed and causing severe bruising. His defence is that the blood had come from his own hand, which he had injured by breaking her glasses, when he hit her. His case and his credibility were collapsing but still he continued his legal battle, funded by the Court of Requests.[54]

Griffith could not provide any witnesses to prove that Marion was trying to stab him, yet witnesses confirmed that Griffith had regularly been physically abusive, and that another associate of Griffith's, John Leach, had hindered Marion's ability to support herself by making cloth. Leach had set his dog loose in Marion and her companions' work area, destroying their completed work and physically threatening them when they objected.

Griffith must have hoped that his own witnesses would strengthen his story. He was, however, to be disappointed. Although one or two cooperated by calling Marion a 'shrew', by and large his witnesses constructed an unflattering image of Griffith as a swindler, a wife-beater and a fraud. After the witness depositions were taken in June 1594, the court heard nothing more from Griffith. He ignored a request to proceed in his case against Marion and her confederates and on 1 February 1595 the case was permanently dismissed from court and Griffith was ordered to pay towards the defendants' legal costs. It is unlikely, from what we know of Griffith Jones's personality, that he ever recompensed his neighbours, but they had successfully escaped any punishment for their role in foiling his plot. The Jones case is a remarkable example of how a neighbourhood could band together to support a wronged wife when the official justice system failed her.

Another husband who used a debt claim to obtain his wife's possessions in a convoluted legal case was Martin Spragin, a tailor from London. In 1595, after nine years of marriage, the couple were separated in the ecclesiastical court due to Spragin's physical abuse of his wife, Joan. Subsequently, the couple drew up a legal document giving Joan a 'reasonable proportion' of their goods, belongings and clothing in order to allow her to survive, permitting her to keep all her earnings after the separation, and guaranteeing her freedom from harassment by her husband. Joan ensured that her husband would fulfil the terms of this agreement by making him sign a bond with a friend of hers, Henry Betts. The terms stated that Martin Spragin would forfeit 100 marks if he did not abide by the terms of their agreement.

After this agreement was entered into, she moved to the house of a man named John Pasmer in Kent. The agreement endured for three years, after which Henry Betts died and Martin Spragin obtained the bond from his widow. Now there was nothing to prevent him from seizing any of his wife's possessions. When his friend, John Allington, filed a claim for a debt of £40, the sheriff of Kent produced a warrant ordering that Joan's possessions should be seized in order to fill this supposed debt. When the bailiffs came, they not only removed all Joan's belongings, but also those of John Pasmer and others residing in the house. Afterwards, another of his confederates, Richard Levens, commenced two suits against Joan, one for slander, and another for assault and battery, with Martin as his primary witness. If these suits succeeded, Joan would have been unable to pay the damages and, consequently, would have been imprisoned.[55]

When Martin Spragin and his associates responded to the complaint, a large chunk of their response was devoted to belittling Joan's social status, describing her as the daughter of a 'poor tapster', instead of responding to the allegations. Afterwards, however, they detailed an intriguing backstory, which was completely absent from Joan's own petition. John Pasmer, with whom she was currently living, had originally been a tenant of both Martin and Joan in London before they had separated. They must have liked each other, as Martin abandoned his former profession as a tailor to run a tavern in Shoreditch called The Ship and Bell in partnership with his wife and John Pasmer. He claimed that they slowly fell into debt and he was forced to borrow money from Pasmer, blaming both Joan's wastefulness and her possible theft of the household funds. Eventually the pub was sold and Spragin returned to his former employment as a tailor. Pasmer was still living with the couple, despite having outstayed his welcome, but eventually left after an argument with Spragin, which the latter attributed to his overfamiliarity.

Pasmer's departure caused an argument between the couple. Martin claimed that Joan had 'protested that she would live and die with… Pasmer and said… that she had rather see him hanged than she would forsake him', after which she departed from the marital home and moved in with her lover. To add insult to injury, Pasmer then had him falsely imprisoned for debt. He claimed that Joan and John Pasmer were having a 'lewd' and 'wicked' affair, which had led them to 'enrich' themselves by 'purloining' his fortune and that the affair had been so obvious that they had been ordered not to cohabit and/or associate, both by the ecclesiastical court and by the sheriff of Kent. Spragin claimed that all this had moved Henry Betts so much that on his deathbed he had freely given Spragin the bond, so that he would no longer be constrained. There had been no plot against Joan.

The court appears to have been confused as to whose version of events was the most accurate. Intriguingly, however, all his witnesses – including Joan's stepfather – gave a very negative account of Martin Spragin's behaviour; all agreed that the couple had initially separated at Martin's insistence because of his jealousy. While accusations of adultery were the easiest way to discharge a husband from any obligations towards a separated wife, it seems odd that Martin would have such specific detail. Many records no longer survive today but in 1595 it would have been a simple matter to write to the judges named and ask them to verify such accounts. The level of detail Martin gave makes it probable that Joan and John Pasmer were indeed having an affair.[56]

Four months later the case had not progressed any further, other than to halt all associated lawsuits. Joan Spragin managed to turn the proceedings around by obtaining witnesses willing to verify her version of events. Numerous witnesses, including their former servants, agreed that Martin was known to be a dishonest man. He was also described as a wife-beater, who beat Joan 'divers and sondry times' and often pawned her clothes for money. They claimed that he had threatened to poison his wife and that they had never heard that Martin was indebted to anyone. An apothecary and grocer named Richard Trout described how he had found Joan at home 'in great extremity of death'. He diagnosed her as a victim of poisoning, implying that Martin was the culprit. An eminent physician, Dr Langton, agreed that she had been poisoned and provided an antidote that seems to have cured her. It cannot have helped his case that Henry Betts's widow, now remarried, flatly denied that her former husband had voluntarily given up the separation bond to Martin Spragin. Instead, she admitted that her current husband had sold Martin the bond for ten shillings, indicating that Martin had lied about at least part of his story.[57]

These allegations seem to have unsettled Martin Spragin and his friends. They started absenting themselves from court, and when the wife of the man who was suing her for slander and assault harangued Joan's lawyer from the witness gallery, calling him a knave, she was consequently imprisoned for disrupting the court. Six months later, in May 1597, the judges appear to have lost patience with them, abruptly demanding that they show the judges proof as to why they should not return Joan and her housemates their belongings. Nearly a year later, however, in January 1598, the court was still reporting that Martin Spragin was refusing to produce any documents requested or to provide witnesses. Either he had been unable to find adequate witnesses, or he knew that his chances of succeeding at this point were slim. It was a long process, but two-and-a-half years later, Joan was awarded damages by the court and Martin was ordered to enter into a new legal agreement that would permanently protect her from any plots or intrigues.[58]

Many women came into court claiming that they had been tricked into marriage for financial gain. Some women stated that they had been lured in by false promises of love by suitors who really had their eyes on the woman's fortune. Others claimed that their husbands had intentionally lied about their own wealth and social status in order to entice them into marriage. The main targets of these schemes were prosperous widows. Not only would they have inherited property, money and goods from their late husband, but they had often been trained in their husband's trade, or to assist in his business. Their independence meant that they were easier targets than young women on their first marriage, who would have been subject to parental and familial controls, and were less likely to possess an independent fortune.

One of the women who claimed to have been tricked was Elizabeth Eggington who, in 1609, had been left land and goods valued at over £40 when her husband Henry Kirkam died. They had been married for just over 20 years when he died, so it seems likely that Elizabeth was in her mid-thirties to early forties. She claimed that she had been approached by her father-in-law, John Eggington, who used 'means and persuasions' to convince her to marry his son, Francis. She married Francis on the basis that his father promised her 'great advancement in marriage', and to award his son property equal to her own as soon as they were married. This clearly was not a love match but a financial arrangement.

The promised rewards, however, did not materialise. Elizabeth portrayed herself as a 'weak and simple woman' who had been duped by a pair of conniving thugs. As soon as the marriage ceremony took place, she found that her husband 'did little regard her'. Both father and son began to use 'wicked and sinister persuasion' to threaten her into surrendering all the property she had inherited from her husband. When she refused to do so, they beat her so severely that she was unable to work. Eventually, she was abducted from her home and driven to the house of her father-in-law, where she was starved to the point that she 'was almost ready to perish for want of food'. She escaped from the house after she was warned that her husband was talking about killing her and burning her corpse in an oven so that she would never be found. Since she had run away, her husband had continued to plunder her property and she had been reduced to begging in the streets to survive. (She was awarded legal aid as a pauper.) He had also installed 'a woman of lewd life and conversation' in the property.[(59)]

As may be expected, the father and son responded by denying that they had mistreated her, or that they had sought to deprive her of her property. What they chose to admit, however, did not portray them in a positive light. They admitted that Francis had rented out her property without her consent, upon which Elizabeth, unsurprisingly, reacted 'in outrage and savage manner', unsettling the tenant to the extent that he was unwilling to remain in the property. Francis Eggington also admitted abducting her, describing how she 'refused, railing and using most vile, bitter and unseemly speeches', that 'with her hands [she] did scratch his face [until] it did bleed', and, somewhat bizarrely, that she had attacked him 'with a wand'.

Although these reactions were understandable, considering that he was abducting her, the Eggingtons attributed Elizabeth's behaviour to a madness gene within her family, saying that her 'father and divers others of her near cousins in blood were lunatic' and that they had died as a result. It is worth asking why Francis Eggington was willing to take his wife back, as he later said that he was, if she was truly the lunatic that he portrayed her to be. Their own account and justification of their behaviour support Elizabeth's claim that they had set out to defraud her.[(60)]

Records in other courts show that Elizabeth had previously been awarded maintenance of 50 shillings by her MP and the local sheriff. The ecclesiastical court had agreed that there was a likelihood of violence towards Elizabeth, forcing both John and Francis Eggington to 'swear the peace' and to pay Elizabeth's legal fees. After this, the records fall silent. When cases disappear abruptly from the records, the most likely outcome was that they reached a deal out of court. The intense levels of personal animosity in this case, however, as well as the previous unresolved legal battles, make this improbable, leaving a question mark over the entire case.

The civil courts could equally fail to help a wife in need of assistance. One of the most shocking cases is that of Holcroft and Elizabeth Blood. The aptly named Holcroft Blood was a violent and sadistic man, who terrorised both his wife and the neighbourhood. His father was a colourful character with a long history of double crossing. He worked (at times simultaneously) for several sides during the Civil War and he took part in several daring wartime rescues, ending with an attempt to steal the Crown Jewels from the Tower of London. After he was caught, he successfully demanded an audience with Charles II, somehow convincing the monarch to set him free. His son, Holcroft, would inherit all of his daring nature, but none of his charm.

In 1686, having failed to distinguish himself in the army, Holcroft married a Catholic widow named Elizabeth Fowler. Her cousin, Richard Biddulph, obtained the army post of Captain of the Pioneers for Holcroft, finally allowing him to shine both in battle and as a military engineer. Even accusations of theft failed to derail his career, and he held three army posts at once as a colonel, lieutenant colonel and engineer general. The Blood marriage, however, had steadily unravelled. Holcroft later described his wife as 'perverse… and ill-natured… much addicted to be angry', while Elizabeth would call him 'more like Nero than a husband'.

It would have been difficult not to be 'ill-natured' when dealing with a man like Holcroft Blood. He started an affair with a friend of the family named Mary Andrews, and invited her to stay overnight at their home frequently, disappearing into her room in the early morning for hours on end. On some occasions the three even went to bed together, with Elizabeth later leaving them alone in the marital bed. Later, Holcroft also asked a neighbour, Dorothy Green, to spend the night with them, attacking her while she was sleeping in the same bed as Elizabeth. When Elizabeth fell seriously ill while they were living at Hornsey, Holcroft refused to fetch her a doctor from London, despite her being in such a 'miserable and despicable condition' that a 'removal might endanger her life'. When his lover's son fell ill, however, Holcroft rode through the night to fetch an apothecary from London.

Elizabeth also accused Holcroft of strangling her until blood gushed out of her ears and of trying to poison her, saying that she had found mercury, then commonly used as a poison, hidden in one of his pockets. While she could not prove this, it fits in with his generally violent nature. Elizabeth finally left the house in a meat cart after 14 years of marriage when he raped her, taking with her a large amount of household goods. She planned to set up a market stall selling eggs, both to support herself and to embarrass her husband by showing that she was forced to sustain herself through lower class work.

After five months of separation, Holcroft tried to persuade his wife to return to the marital home, presumably because she was running up large debts and encouraging her creditors to sue her husband for payment. Elizabeth had been living in hiding since she had left, so Holcroft asked a friend of hers to arrange a meeting to discuss their marital problems. However, the situation quickly deteriorated when Elizabeth, understandably, lost her temper and started to call him names such as 'rogue' and 'dog'. When she finally refused to come home, saying that she feared he would kill her, he gave her a final punch over her ear, knocking her down. Enraged, Holcroft then began punching her in the face, causing such a commotion that people burst into the room and a large crowd gathered outside, including a constable called by a neighbour. Immediately after the assault, with blood from her nose running down into her mouth, she in turn had spat out the blood into Holcroft's face.

Two days later, when she appeared before the judge, she was still 'black and blue, from the lower part of her forehead almost to her mouth, her eyes black and swelled, and she had clots of blood in one of her ears'. The constable was asked to take Holcroft before a magistrate, so that Elizabeth could indict him for assault but he refused to go, on the grounds that a husband could discipline his wife as he wished. Not only was Holcroft an intimidating man personally, he also had a high social position as a wealthy army officer and the constable did not have the strength to defy him. Elizabeth had to make her own way to court, despite her severe injuries.

She had the misfortune to appear before Justice Thomas Boteler, a personal friend of Holcroft's barrister brother, Charles. He refused to issue any warrants before talking to Charles Blood, presumably hoping to convince the family to sort the matter out privately. However, Charles Blood gave Justice Boteler two legal documents signed by another magistrate and Blood family friend, blocking any summons that Boteler might issue, on the grounds that another court, the Quarter Sessions, was already dealing with the case, and that Holcroft had already given a financial guarantee to the court that he would attend when summoned. In fact, these documents were not genuine. Holcroft had pulled strings and called in favours to avoid being prosecuted for assault.

The marriage was obviously at an end, for Holcroft was not going to change his violent nature, and Elizabeth was no longer content to suffer in silence. He was clearly not going to give her any maintenance that would have been considered adequate by a court. He took the precaution of claiming that he was in debt to a friend for the entire amount of his estate, leaving nothing for Elizabeth to live on, saying 'I [do not] owe anything, you know; it is but to trick the law'. He also threatened that if she continued to try and have him called before the magistrates for assault, he would obtain false witnesses to swear that they had seen her having sex with both a dog and a horse. She rejected all his separation proposals, which ranged from her entering a nunnery to colluding to have the marriage falsely annulled by an ecclesiastical court on the grounds that one of them had been pre-contracted (ie engaged) to another person. As Elizabeth refused all his suggestions, he refused to give her the proposed allowance, and negotiations collapsed.

She was left with no choice but to sue Holcroft for a legal separation herself on the grounds of cruelty and adultery. She was awarded a maintenance allowance while the case progressed but was unable to provide any evidence for his adultery, or other claims that he was practising sodomy. Holcroft, on the other hand, produced a wide range of character witnesses, who testified that he was a 'gentleman, a man of honour, courteous and civil in his Carriage, peaceable and quiet, quick in his humour and conversation and obliging to all persons'. The court records show a frequent repetition of their surname, Blood, which is not seen in other cases, and it may be that Elizabeth was trying to hint that Holcroft came from a violent family. The assault, however, was excused on the grounds that Elizabeth had provoked him to beat her.

A rare positive sign came when a bailiff called about an unpaid debt to a milliner and she directed him to Holcroft's address instead. It looked as if she had finally secured a victory, but the case collapsed as her sudden increase in expenditure indicated that she had been intentionally extravagant in a bid to ruin Holcroft. The worst moment came when Holcroft produced witnesses who testified that Elizabeth had been seen living with another man as his wife six months previously. Elizabeth's case was shattered, as the contemporary legal code held that her alleged adultery meant that she could not object to Holcroft's, as they had both sinned equally. As an adulteress, she was also not entitled to any maintenance.

Elizabeth fought back, appealing to a higher court and producing her own witnesses who testified that she had been living with them when she had supposedly been living with a lover. She also organised an early identity parade, where the witnesses to her supposed adultery were asked to identify her from a group of seven women. They all failed to do so. This, together with Holcroft's long pattern of legal trickery, makes it exceedingly likely that this was a plot to deprive Elizabeth of her separation allowance.

Unfortunately, he was successful. Elizabeth received her legal separation but she had no claim upon Holcroft's estate, in an example of how social position, money and a cunning nature could completely destroy a case for separation, even when there were multiple witnesses to a brutal assault. When Holcroft died two years later, his mistress was given an income of £100 a year and all his valuable goods while Elizabeth was given a one-off payment of 40 shillings. Elizabeth Blood may have been both forceful and resourceful but these qualities did not always win the day.[61]

Another occasion where alimony was denied on the basis that the wife had been unfaithful occurred in 1562. Sir Humfrey Stafford successfully argued that his estranged wife, Elizabeth Stafford, had forfeited her rights by committing adultery. Lady Stafford seems to have petitioned the court for maintenance, but her husband submitted a lengthy statement detailing why he was not obliged to comply. This centred on his claim that she had committed adultery with various men, which he described as 'her naughty living'. He said that Elizabeth was 'notoriously known to have lived an inconvenient life and adulterously with... Thomas Butler but also with dyvers others... one Robert Brown, gentleman and one Thomas Bent, sometime servant' to Lord Stafford. On multiple occasions, Lady Stafford and Thomas Butler would order the servants to leave them alone together. Afterwards, the servants would investigate only to find the imprint of two bodies in the bed, which naturally led to servant gossip. The couple would also separate from a hunting group, hiding in a bush from the rest of the party.

After Butler departed the household, she was seen canoodling with a man named Robert Brown and seeking out places 'to accomplish their carnal devilish determination'. Not only was Brown seen standing semi-naked in her bedroom, but he admitted the affair on his deathbed, saying that they had had sex frequently, up to six times a night, 'whereof also he took his death immediately, without recanting or repenting'. Brown's uncle and two of his relatives later testified to this confession, and other details of 'their filthy conversation, their adulterous and carnal copulation' in the ecclesiastical court.

Lady Stafford's closest emotional entanglement appears to have occurred after the death of Robert Brown with, perhaps most shockingly to the court, a servant named Thomas Bent. She was seen sneaking off to his quarters in the middle of the night and she invited him to spend hours talking and eating together in her rooms. She even said that she would not continue cohabiting with her husband if he dismissed Thomas from his service. Sir Humfrey accused the couple of embezzling money from his estate, which Bent could well have done in his position as steward of the Stafford estates. After Bent failed to explain how he was disposing of Sir Humfrey's money to his satisfaction, he turned Bent over to the Chief Justice of the King's Bench, Sir Roger Cholmley. Uncovering 'sondry false practices' led

Sir Roger to imprison Bent in a debtor's prison, after which Elizabeth Stafford left the house.

Her reputation was in ruins. Sir Humfrey explained that he could not venture into company without having her behaviour mentioned, either openly mocked or discussed behind his back. During the course of the ecclesiastical suit, Elizabeth attempted to clear her name by performing a purgation ritual. This was where an accused person, either male or female, would take an oath that they were innocent of the charges brought against them, supported by neighbours who would also affirm that they believed that the accused was innocent. Elizabeth Stafford ran into problems, however, when all the highborn ladies and gentlemen of the area refused to support her purgation. She was forced to ask relatives who lived elsewhere to support her oath, and she made sure that she took the oath as far away from her home as possible. Neither did she notify the local community by announcing the date in the parish church, as she was supposed to do. This came to nothing anyway, as Lady Stafford made a disastrous error. In the presence of high ranking officials she had gone 'down of her knees [and] submitted herself to the said defendant [Lord Stafford] and to him declared at large her incontinent living and with whom and how often'.

Upon this evidence she was divorced from bed and board from Sir Humfrey in the ecclesiastical court, under such circumstances that Sir Humfrey was 'not bound by any law at his cost or charges to relieve, sustain or maintain her'. Legal proceedings seem to have stopped here.[62] This demonstrates that certain standards of behaviour, including chastity, had to be adhered to in order to maintain a wife's rights to the support of legal institutions after her separation.

In the vast majority of separation cases where female adultery was involved, the participants were of the same social class. In an era where social status defined every detail of people's lives, very few women would have risked degrading themselves and eroding their authority as a mistress by indulging in an affair with a servant, openly or otherwise.

One notable exception, apart from Lady Stafford, was Clara Louisa Middleton. She had seemingly been happily married to her husband

William for more than ten years when a new groom, John Rose, was hired at their home, Stockeld Park. She spent more time with Rose than would perhaps have been customary. He was detailed to follow alongside her when she went riding, instead of maintaining the more usual respectful distance behind her, as Clara Louisa had had several riding accidents in the past. This level of increased contact seems to have led to her developing a noticeable crush on John Rose.

Initially the servants kept silent but it soon grew too obvious to ignore and rumours began to spread outside the household. Both visiting and household servants noticed that she watched Rose constantly whenever he was in the room, with one visiting servant commenting: 'Surely your mistress must be in love with him, as she never had her eyes off him the whole time of dinner'. Another visiting servant grew so bold as to communicate the rumours to their mistress, who also started observing the couple.

Real evidence of the affair, however, only came six months later, when people noticed that John Rose was suddenly richly dressed in silk with silver shoe buckles. He had arrived in very 'low and distressed circumstances' and this sudden change in fortune aroused people's suspicion. Clara Louisa was observed buying gifts, such as a pocket watch, with her pin money, instead of charging it to the house account as she normally did. Later John Rose would be seen with these items. Mistress and groom were observed by a variety of witnesses standing very close to each other, kissing, holding hands and placing their arms around the other. Suspicion was further aroused when Clara Louisa started taking walks after dinner, alone and in the dark no matter how bad the weather. She was followed, only to be found meeting Rose. She would return to the house with the back of her dress covered in dirt, indicating that she had been lying on the ground.

Most of the blame was thrust upon Clara Louisa. It was assumed that she had made the first move by expressing 'great love and affection for him and made other familiar advances', as no servant would have dared take the liberty. It is difficult to tell whether people were more disgusted that the couple were having an adulterous relationship, or the fact that the affair had crossed social boundaries.

One servant, William Hodgson, confronted Clara Louisa, saying: 'You ought to be ashamed of acknowledging an attachment for him who is only a stable boy'. They were clearly worried that they had been observed in some illicit act, as immediately after this conversation, John Rose pulled the servant to one side and gave him a guinea to keep quiet. On other occasions, Clara Louisa was urged by servants to leave the area for a prolonged period, either to visit friends or to go to one of the fashionable holiday spots of the time such as Bath, in the hope that distance would cure her of the infatuation.

Clara Louisa could not bring herself to let John go, though, or to go herself, and continued to make the affair obvious by buying him expensive presents. Her infatuation for John Rose had completely taken her over to the point that discretion and logic could no longer play a part in her thinking. She confessed to a servant: 'I love him above all others. I never knew what love was until I knew him', and on another occasion: 'I have everything that... [my] heart could wish but one, which is to marry John, which I never can'.

Rumours about the entanglement had started to become common knowledge and great efforts were necessary if they were to avoid a scandal. Clara Louisa seems to have believed that the best form of defence was a strong attack. She forced Hodgson to retract his story publicly in front of other servants, 'in a strange, uncommon, stammering, silly manner'. She then told her husband, who had been living in ignorance of the affair, that the servants were making false accusations against her, which he accepted without question, advising her to dismiss them all. Assured of her husband's support, she called in one of the leading tenants and burst into tears, declaring her innocence.

These were clever moves, and if Clara Louisa had let Rose depart at this point, it is likely that nothing further would have come of the affair. But she didn't and eventually they were observed by the wrong person, a maid named Hannah Canridge. The servants, loyal to Clara Louisa, who had so far done their best to dissolve the affair, had set up a surveillance network designed to make it more difficult for the couple to meet. Hannah later wrote that 'every servant in the house knows it and is constantly watching her' in an attempt to hinder and conceal the affair. One day it was Hannah's turn to follow Clara Louisa but the couple were not in the stables as she expected. She was called back to the house by three sharp whistles, where she was told that the couple had gone for a walk. She set off in hot pursuit, finding John Rose with his arm around her mistress's waist. Hannah threatened to tell William Middleton of the affair and demanded that John Rose should leave the household. He agreed, but when he tried to leave two days later, Clara Louisa collapsed in hysterics, claiming that she could not let him go and threatening to commit suicide.

Hannah had seen this pattern enacted too many times, however, and she prepared to take action. When William Middleton's brother Maxwell arrived for a Christmas visit in 1792, he found a letter in his room, written by Hannah, informing him that Clara Louisa had 'an unfortunate affection for the groom' and that she was refusing to end the affair. He intervened that night, ordering John Rose to leave the house. When Clara Louisa found that he had gone, she fired Hannah and then had what appears to be a nervous breakdown.

Hannah wrote later that Clara 'wished Hell to open and swallow us up, she wished us so tortured too with all sorts of plagues all the days of eternity'. Clara raved: 'Damned villain and that eternal bitch, you have banished him… I must never see him more'. She galloped after him in an attempt to find him but was unsuccessful. She returned so distraught that the servants spent the night with her on suicide watch. Hannah and another servant, Robert Malthus, were dismissed with no wages and no references to obtain another position, destroying both their lives.

William Middleton recalled John Rose to Stockeld and for a while, it seemed as though life would go on as before. The remaining servants were too scared to intervene, fearing that they too would be dismissed with their career in tatters. It seems, however, that William's suspicions were finally aroused. Shortly after Hannah and Robert's departure, the butler, Baldwin, had also left, presumably to avoid being caught up in another of Clara Louisa's machinations. His replacement, William Davis, must have seemed bizarre to the remaining servants. He was a man with a rather chequered career, part servant, part farmer. Whenever Davis had previously worked as a servant, he had either been dismissed for insolence or had left the household after a blazing row. He had a reputation as a 'suspicious, malicious person, in the habit of making and circulating reports against the characters of women'. In short, he was a strange choice as a butler but perfect as a watchdog for Clara Louisa. A love triangle then formed with the arrival of Hannah Canridge's replacement, Hester Swinburne, which would spark off another set of events at Stockeld. While Davis fell in love with her, she in turn fell for John Rose, who appears to have pursued several of the maids at Stockeld simultaneously, while profiting from his affair with the mistress.

The matter could still have been concealed if Clara Louisa had exercised more caution. On the night of Easter Saturday, however, John Rose was seen by two servants making his way to the upper storey, and they heard one of the bedroom doors click open. He could either have been heading to Clara Middleton or Hester Swinburne's bedroom. John Davis, inflamed by jealousy, assumed that Rose had spent the night with Hester Swinburne and accused him of doing so the next day. Meanwhile, tensions were building downstairs, with Hester upset at being accused. When the cook, Jean Bouvier, repeated this accusation, she responded by hurling abuse and cups of tea at him, instigating a physical fight that Davis had to break up.

There was evidence, however, that John had spent the night with Clara Louisa instead. When the housemaids went to make her bed, they saw that it had been slept in by two people. Simultaneously, Davis, perhaps feeling guilty at the uproar his accusations had caused downstairs, started to suspect that he may not have been correct. He publicly apologised to Hester, saying that it was unlikely that John would have slept with her when he could have slept with the mistress.

When William returned from London, Davis, stretching the truth, told him that Rose had been seen entering Clara Louisa's bedroom. William immediately summoned his lawyers to Stockeld to interrogate the servants, recalled the old servants he had dismissed, and ordered Clara Louisa to leave the house immediately without any of her belongings or children. William Middleton is almost absent from the early part of this narrative but he emerges as a man not to be trifled with once he realises that Clara Louisa has been lying. He has her horse shot and her dog hanged, simply because she loved them. The children were similarly removed to boarding school. William also soon left Stockeld, unable to cope with the memories.

The servants split into two camps: those who had provided evidence for William and knew their livelihood now depended on the permanent break-up of the marriage, and those who had helped Clara Louisa conceal the affair, and were summarily dismissed when they refused to provide evidence.

Clara Louisa took a forceful role in representing herself. The court records show that she often 'appeared personally' and instructions were often written 'in her own handwriting'. Davis was particularly vehement in bullying those whom he suspected were hiding information from the lawyers. The stable boy Thomas Birkenshaw, was beaten in an attempt to make him talk, and Davis struck one old villager, William Greaves, when he refused to give evidence against the couple.

Clara Louisa, however, supported by her family, was exceptionally effective in rewarding servants who stood by her. Some were offered employment with either Clara or her family, others were financially rewarded so substantially that they were able to marry after years of courtship. Those who had been physically threatened were spirited away to Ireland, as was John Rose himself. William Middleton in his turn also rewarded those who provided him with evidence.

Despite his financial power, William Middleton ran into numerous obstacles when he attempted to sue for separation on the grounds of adultery. Many witnesses 'refused... to attend and give their testimony, unless by Law compelled thereunto' and bailiffs had to be ordered to deliver the witnesses' official summons. Clara Louisa's lawyer suggested that 'his party would be better relieved by the answers' of William Middleton, seeing as he seemed to be the only person who had grounds to suspect her. Despite the abundance of suggestive evidence, no one could swear that they had seen any physical act of adultery take place. This obstacle might have been overcome by an interrogation of John Rose but he could not be found. William therefore set out to destroy Clara Louisa's reputation while attempting to trick her into admitting her guilt. He conveyed a series of verbal and written offers of forgiveness to Clara Louisa, conditional on her admitting her guilt. When these offers were rejected, articles appeared in the *Bon Ton* magazine, written by a friend of William's mother, falsely describing how Clara Louisa and John Rose had been caught committing adultery in the stables.

She fought off every attempt at attack, no matter how much money or legal trickery was behind it, suing the publishers of the *Bon Ton* for libel. Belief in her innocence was widespread throughout society. When she gave birth to a child conceived just before her banishment from Stockeld, both the Earl of Fingall and the Countess of Shrewsbury stood as godparents at the baptism. When she travelled back to Stockeld to gather more evidence, the villagers met her carriage, unhitched the horses and drew the carriage into town. This was followed by rallies in her favour, where effigies of her accusers were burned. When one accuser travelled into town, he was pelted with rotten eggs. Support for Clara Louisa was clearly riding high at all social levels.

Two years after legislation had first begun, Clara Louisa was surprisingly secure for a woman accused of adultery. She had been awarded a comfortable alimony of £600 a year while the case was being heard, she enjoyed the support of all sections of society, and after publicly commenting on the defects of the original case, the judge was preparing to acquit her. If she had waited a while longer to see John Rose, it is exceedingly likely that she would have won.

But after two years, her infatuation was as strong as ever. In the summer of 1794, thinking herself safe, she summoned John Rose from Ireland to meet her at Littlehampton where she was staying with friends. At first they took care to try and avoid attention, meeting on roads as if by chance, yet as time went on they grew more comfortable, openly kissing and holding hands. Reports soon spread, reaching the ears of her friends, the Dorsets. At first she attempted to deny the accusations, but when three witnesses were produced willing to testify to what they had seen, she broke down, saying: 'My God... I shall be ruined in both character and fortune'. Unbelievably, however, the Dorsets supported her and did not reveal her secret. Someone must have also paid off local residents to avoid revealing the secret.

This must have emboldened her to bring John Rose to London, setting him up in lodgings near Tottenham Court Road under an assumed name. His landlord later testified that Clara Louisa often visited John under the pretence that she was his sister. On one occasion he saw Rose exchanging kisses for money, revealing a good deal about his motivations and the balance of power within the relationship. Rose's true identity was exposed when he was seen by a shoemaker from Yorkshire, whose master had made shoes for the Middletons before Stockeld Park was closed. The shoemaker went straight to William's brother, who had legal documents ready and waiting to summon Rose to court. When he was served, Rose stupidly admitted to the landlord that his 'sister' was not actually his sister, and that it was 'about her that they are making all this bustle'.

The game was over, John Rose was sued for £10,000 in damages, the equivalent of more than £500,000 today, for committing adultery with another man's wife, and he was imprisoned to await trial. Clara Louisa's solicitor was able to argue the awarded damages down to £561 and costs, but both she and John Rose were formally convicted of adultery and William Middleton was consequently awarded his legal separation. Both Rose and Clara Louisa largely disappear from records at this stage but it is unlikely that they lived happily after the case was concluded. The relationship appears to have been founded largely on money, with a desperate Clara Louisa providing money for John Rose in return for affection. Clara Louisa was faced with a drastically reduced income of £100 once her guilt was proven and the court awarded maintenance was withdrawn. Once the money disappeared, there would have been little reason for John to stay; there is no evidence to suggest that he had any genuine affection for Clara Louisa. On her part, she cannot have been happy to hear evidence of his other affairs and that he was infected with a venereal disease. The lack of evidence that Clara Louisa was infected with any kind of sexually transmitted disease makes it likely that full intercourse had not taken place, but there had clearly been a physical element to the affair.[63]

Knowing how strong and pervasive patriarchy could be, and how it constrained women's lives, it can be difficult for us to believe that there was any help for unhappy wives in England in the past. Yet there are enough examples to show that the law would not always support a husband. Some women managed to use the legal system to great effect. In theory, no court had the right to withhold a wife's earnings from her husband, but we have seen that in Tudor England courts would actually do so. In the sixteenth and seventeenth century, when the law was less centralised and more dependent on a judge's personal opinion, legal theory could be discarded to provide a woman with the protection and/or resources that he felt necessary. As time went on, this would become considerably more difficult for women.

Other women, such as Elizabeth Blood, found themselves thwarted. Despite being forceful and dynamic, she was not strong enough to overcome the social and financial power of her husband. These very qualities may have been enough to turn a judge against her. Throughout this period, access to legal support was dependent on women adhering to male expectations of virtue and chastity. Women convicted of adultery, for example, could expect little, if any, help from a court. From Elizabeth Stafford in the sixteenth century to Clara Louisa in the early nineteenth century, wives would be left penniless if there was evidence of any adulterous activity. There are stories the records cannot tell us. When a case was dropped for whatever reason, as with Elizabeth Eggington, the records simply frustratingly stop.

Similarly, we cannot always learn how many women had problems enforcing their maintenance payments. It is also difficult to know how aware women were of their right to legal recourse. Women had access to legal aid but we cannot tell how many women were aware that a court might pay for their expenses or indeed give them any protection. Marion Jones, for example, only appears in records due to her husband's penchant for litigation. If he had not sued her, she would have received her justice through her local community, who turned out in numbers to try and protect her from harm. It seems likely that most women received their justice through these informal communities, rather than using the court system. It is encouraging to know that there were informal institutions prepared to protect mistreated women, even in those patriarchal times.

CHAPTER 4

Separation Agreements:
A Disagreeable Situation

' I have only to hope that this case may prove a warning to any woman… It is to be hoped that the time may not be far distant when there will be… some law passed for the better protection of the interests of women'.[64] This was the last will and testament of Emily, Marchioness of Westmeath. Her legal battle to enforce her separation deed dragged on for years, leaving her resentful of both the English legal system and patriarchal restrictions. Many other women, however, found that a separation deed could guarantee a wife personal and financial freedom. A separation agreement was a middle ground between an informal separation and a parliamentary divorce. Until 1677, this was the most formal and official method of marital separation available to a couple. They became increasingly popular from the eighteenth century onwards.

A separation agreement could provide a wife with financial security and protection from threats. Deeds were drawn up with the assistance of friends and/or lawyers, formalising the separation, providing the lady with an income and guaranteeing her freedom from harassment. If the agreements were not followed, the courts could order maintenance payments and enforce early forms of restraining orders. Legal separations could also be settled privately, through agreements that were drawn up between the couple themselves.

One example of a separation agreement is the 1747 legal deed drawn up for Mary and Robert Poyntz. The agreement awarded Mary maintenance 'for her sole proper and separate use Exclusive of the said Robert Poyntz her Husband and to be disposed of by her in such manner as she shall think proper'. This type of agreement guaranteed a wife an income independent of any harassment from her former husband. There were, furthermore, formal guarantees which could extend to her living arrangements. One sample clause, again from the separation agreement of Robert and Mary Poyntz, states that:

> the said Mary his wife shall and may without any Suit, Hindrance, Interruption, Complaint, Molestation or Trouble whatsoever of or by the said Robert Poyntz or any person or persons whatsoever of, by or with his Direction... live separate and apart from him... with any person or persons and in such place and places as the said Mary his wife shall think fit.

The deed further goes on to affirm that Robert Poyntz:

> shall not nor will at any time or times hereafter... by any Process from any Ecclesiastical Court or otherwise enforce or compel the said Mary his wife to live and cohabit with him or... molest her or disturb her for not so doing or bring suit or prosecute against her or against any person or persons whatsoever for or on account of... their receiving, harbouring, entertaining, detaining, or assisting his said wife.[65]

Women appear to have had a great deal of input into these agreements. Men figure prominently in negotiations – Mary Poyntz had her trustees and Elizabeth Bourne had her associates – to argue on their behalves. Many women, however, kept a firm hand on the reins. The letters of Elizabeth, Duchess of Kingston, to her friend and negotiator the Earl of Barrington, demonstrate how determined she was not to lose control of the process, despite her obvious trust in him. The Duchess had been secretly married in her youth to the future Earl of Bristol but it had, at that time, been deemed expedient to hide the marriage, and then to pretend it had never happened. She had been accepted as the wife and widow of the Duke of Kingston until she was convicted of bigamy. Now, her first husband, the Earl of Bristol, was attempting to obtain his own ecclesiastical separation from the Duchess.

Although the Duchess asks the Earl of Barrington to meet her first husband and obtain information regarding his 'proposals', she gives frequent directions for these meetings. The Duchess is the one to decide when and whether the Earl 'would have an interview with him'.[66] She also directed him to focus on certain matters. One letter implores him to see 'what security I might have for my fortune... there is an answer but I must see that security and approve it'.[67] Furthermore, she clearly retains the ability to decide whether or not his terms are acceptable. Lord Barrington is directed 'always to excuse yourself from coming to a conclusion until I return'.[68] The Duchess would be the one making the final decision as to whether or not Lord Bristol's proposals are acceptable.

The Duchess seems to have been at least somewhat successful. Although she did not manage to prevent the separation, the Earl complained that 'I have met with nothing but Chicane, delays and Expense from giving every delay they [the Duchess and her lawyers] could'.[69] Clearly, the Duke felt that the Duchess herself had been successful in throwing up obstacles and delaying the proceedings, as opposed to her friends and/or lawyers. Wives of high social status, who were most likely to use these separation agreements, were well placed to argue with their husbands. This demonstrates three things. Firstly, that wives were able to exercise agency by consulting lawyers regarding their agreements. Secondly, that wives were able to refuse their separated husband's demands. Thirdly, these agreements were seen as binding, both by those who wrote them and those who signed them.

One of the first cases where a separation agreement was used was that of Sir Oliver and Anne, Lady Boteler, who married in 1656. Sir Oliver was abusive both 'in word and deed' over a period of seven years. Lady Boteler, on the other hand, was described as a 'very obedient wife to him, a modest person... observant and dutiful'. He was seen beating his wife, punching her and throwing chairs at her. He would deliberately target her stomach while she was pregnant, causing her to miscarry on at least one occasion. He even dragged her along the ground round the house, holding her by her dress. Sir Oliver also directed his rage towards their children, beating them all so severely that they could not move for days and on one occasion threatening to drop their daughter down the stairs. When he wasn't hitting them, he was teaching them to beat their mother and spit in her face.

He terrorised Lady Boteler psychologically, forcing her to lie face down on the floor while calling her his 'domestic servant', a tremendous insult at that time for someone of high social status. He made her carry out menial chores, such as fetching him chamber pots. He discharged all her servants, forcing her to dress herself and care for the children – this at a time when the gentry spent little time with their children and did not interest themselves with their day-to-day care. He especially targeted Lady Boteler when she was in a 'weak condition' after giving birth. He treated her in a 'barbarous manner', throwing her clothes in the fire despite it being the middle of winter, and forbidding the servants to bring her any of their own clothes. He also tried to force her to have sex with him while the servants were watching.

The final blow came in 1670 when Anne became infected with a sexually transmitted disease. Sir Oliver was sleeping with several different women at the same time and he contracted gonorrhoea, also infecting his wife. An argument ensued as to who had infected who and Sir Oliver threatened to refuse to sleep with Anne again, something that was unlikely to have caused her too much anxiety. What would have distressed her, though, were his threats to disinherit the children and leave his estate to one of his illegitimate children, rendering them penniless. The servants restrained him from attacking Anne but he continued to threaten her, saying: 'I will lock you in a dark hole and feed you with bread and water'. Anne ran away to her mother-in-law's house, where her children were already residing. However, when she was tricked into returning, Sir Oliver locked her away and threatened to kill her in a way that would leave no mark. Anne made her escape a second time, most likely aided by the servants, and she never returned.

SEPARATION AGREEMENTS

Her troubles, however, were not over, as Anne faced the problem of survival outside the marital home. She had been granted an income of £650 a year after Sir Oliver's death but there had been no provision of a separate income while he was alive. Sir Oliver's stepfather, Sir Philip Warwick, arranged a separation deed granting Anne an income of £300 a year and somehow convinced Sir Oliver to sign. She lived for two years in relative peace until her protector and mother-in-law, Lady Warwick, died and Sir Oliver sued for a restitution of conjugal rights. Anne was left with no choice but to countersue for a separation and alimony on the grounds of cruelty. The case dragged on for three years while Anne battled for an increase in her maintenance and her trustees fought on her behalf to make Sir Oliver follow the separation deed. In the end, however, they were successful. Anne had not only her separation and her maintenance but also, in a move that would have been unthinkable a century later, she was awarded custody of her daughter until her marriage. It is to be hoped that this finally brought her a degree of tranquillity towards the end of a turbulent and brutal life.

Unusually, the family servants all testified on Anne's behalf, confirming all her claims of abuse and describing how, when Sir Oliver came home drunk, they had to hide all the weapons to stop him from injuring her. In an unparalleled move, a servant had even removed the children from the house without authorisation when Sir Oliver threatened to kill them. Sir Oliver's mother and stepfather also supported Anne throughout the case.

Many of the attacks seem to have been triggered by alcohol, and it is probable that Sir Oliver had a recognised drinking problem that led his family to withdraw support. One of the beatings was due to her refusal to join him in a drinking session. There also may have been pre-existing mental problems. He once told her that: 'I hate you the more because you love me so well, and I will never leave till I have broken your heart'. Thanks to this separation agreement, Lady Anne managed to escape her abusive marriage.[70]

Another, less innocent lady, who also used the legal system multiple times to defeat her abusive husband was the Countess of Strathmore, an ancestor of Queen Elizabeth II through the Queen Mother. Born

Mary Eleanor Bowes, she had inherited a large fortune from her father (estimated to be worth around £100 million today). She married the Earl of Strathmore when she was 18, giving birth to five children, but the marriage was not a happy one. He derided her literary ambitions, and forced her to give up socialising in intellectual circles. She took an 'unnatural dislike' to her sons, especially her eldest, and continued flirting with various men after her marriage. Her primary 'headstrong passion' was for a man named James Graham, with whom she communicated through his sister. On the rare occasion that letters were sent, Mary Eleanor burned them and mixed the ashes with water, which she then drank.

Her only physical affair, however, was with an entrepreneur named George Gray, who fortuitously propositioned her just after she was told that James Graham was paying court to a lady in Minorca. Initially as a form of revenge, she started to meet Gray in Kensington Gardens and Hyde Park, progressing to meetings at her house in Grosvenor Square. When Lord Strathmore set sail for Portugal in 1776, the affair intensified and despite the 'precautions' that they took, Mary Eleanor found herself pregnant. She must have been unable to pass the child off as Lord Strathmore's, as she became 'so frightened and unhappy by it' that she asked Gray to bring her a 'quack medicine' used as a means of inducing miscarriages. Mary Eleanor used the 'black, inky kind of substance' to induce two miscarriages in 1776. The third time it failed, and in desperation Mary Eleanor drank a queer mixture of brandy, pepper and a substance designed to make her vomit, which apparently terminated her third pregnancy that year.

On 7 March 1776, however, Lord Strathmore died off the coast of Lisbon and Mary Eleanor was free. Six months later, she went through a secret betrothal ceremony at St Paul's Cathedral. After this legally binding ceremony, Mary Eleanor laid plans to marry Gray in the spring, a barely respectable year after Lord Strathmore's death, and embark on an extended trip round Europe, giving any scandal time to die down. Once the gossips had forgotten them, Mary Eleanor and her new husband would return to England, where she would assume her former social position.[71]

SEPARATION AGREEMENTS

We would expect Mary Eleanor to have married George Gray and lived happily ever after, but this did not happen. The first reason was, as we shall see later, that George Gray was not in love with Mary Eleanor. The second, and most important reason, was an adventurer named Andrew Stoney, who was attractive, charismatic and utterly ruthless. Stoney's first marriage was to an heiress, whom he had terrorised so badly (even by eighteenth century standards), that it had become the talk of Durham. One observer called him a 'brute and a savage', and reported that he was both physically and emotionally abusive. On one occasion 'he locked his wife in a closet, that would barely contain her, for three days in her chemise... and fed her with an egg a day' and on another he threw her down the stairs at a public meeting. He 'knew secret ways of provoking her before company', and when she reacted to his baiting, used this as evidence of her unsatisfactory nature. Legal trusts meant that when she died (four days after the Earl of Strathmore), without a living child, her fortune reverted to her family of origin, not Stoney. He was in need of a new, rich wife and Mary Eleanor was the biggest prize on the marriage market.

The fact that her affair with Gray had become the talk of the town and newspapers were attacking her with 'illiberal abuse' in the expectation that the couple were to marry would have deterred any other man. Stoney, however, moved to London, took up lodgings near Grosvenor Square and started paying court to Mary Eleanor, while forming bonds with her children's governess and long-term friend, Eliza Planta. He made profusions of love and pretended to be fascinated by all her interests, coached by Eliza. Mary Eleanor was flattered and encouraged him as she had encouraged countless others, but her first loyalty was to George Gray and she continued planning for their wedding. Stoney realised that stronger measures were needed and he hatched a plan so cunning that it continues to reverberate throughout the centuries.

His first move was so outrageous that, if it were fiction, it would be dismissed as ludicrous. He told Eliza to suggest that they, along with another friend of Stoney's, visit a fortune teller near Newgate Prison.

When the fortune teller accurately described Stoney and the important role he would play in Mary Eleanor's future, despite her disguise as a grocer's widow, she must have been favourably impressed. She could not know that the whole outing had been engineered by Stoney, with Eliza Planta's connivance. This visit was quickly followed by a fake letter from a supposed jilted lover of Stoney's, asking Mary Eleanor to marry Gray quickly so that Stoney would return to her, and casually mentioning that Gray had been negotiating a truce with enemies of Mary Eleanor's within Lord Strathmore's family. Taken in, Mary Eleanor was upset that Gray would seek peace with the Lyon family, as Stoney knew she would be, and it helped to sow a seed of discontent in the relationship. But the affair continued and, for the fourth time that year, Mary Eleanor found she was pregnant with Gray's child. This time, the abortifacients did not work. At the same time, articles appeared in the *Morning Post* attacking her, arguing that she had disgraced her husband's memory by her affair with Gray and had abandoned her children. They read exactly as if the information had come from one of the late Lord Strathmore's family, the Lyons.

When Stoney vowed to defend Mary Eleanor's honour, and challenged the editor of the *Morning Post* to a duel, she was thrilled, going so far as to bless the sword and take it to bed with her. She had always delighted in grand, romantic gestures and this occasion was no different. It is doubtful, however, whether she expected things to go as far as they did. Stoney met the editor at the Turk's Head coffee house on the Strand on 10 January 1667, where they proceeded to fire without wounding each other. It is curious that Stoney was not successful. His proximity to the target and his military training indicate that he may have botched the shot on purpose. Honour would have been satisfied at this point but Stoney insisted on continuing until they were both wounded. Mary Eleanor was informed the next day by no less than three medical men that Stoney was dying. She immediately went to visit him where, as his final request, Stoney asked her to marry him, so that he could die as her husband. She was reluctant but, assured that he was truly dying, from what she later described as a 'misapplied sense of Gratitude and Honour', she did indeed marry him at St James's Church in Piccadilly. As he was carried up the aisle, 'in a constant state of agitation' until he made his vows, Mary Eleanor had no reason to suspect that the marriage would last any longer than a few days.

Yet it did. Servants would later testify that Stoney's shirt showed no evidence of wounds, much less of participating in a duel. Other witnesses later admitted that makeup had been used to create Stoney's deathly pallor. It had all been an ingenious plot and Mary Eleanor, pregnant with another man's child, was unexpectedly trapped in a marriage she had undertaken out of pity, and which she had expected to end almost immediately. Nor was George Gray willing to help her. Once he learned of the wedding, and Andrew Stoney's miraculous survival, he understandably reacted with anger, threatening to sue her for breach of promise. Stoney and Mary Eleanor raised the impressive sum of £12,000 to stop this suit, and a placated George Gray left Mary Eleanor to her fate, dying in Bengal two years later.

A rapidly recovered Stoney then started to abuse his new wife. One onlooker would later write, 'the iron rod of her tyrant had despoiled her of her charms, broken down her spirit, wasted her body, and eclipsed her faculties'. She was beaten, pinched, kicked, slapped and once was chased around a room with a sword. Many of her old servants left, disgusted with Stoney's behaviour. Stoney was slightly disconcerted to learn that she was pregnant with another man's child but he was apoplectic when he found out that Mary Eleanor had taken steps to protect her fortune. In preparation for her marriage to Gray, she had signed a deed stating that her income could only be used by her, independent of any future husband. After failing to get her trustees to surrender this deed, he forced her to sign a paper revoking the deed, and handing over all control to him.

The physical abuse continued, but now Stoney refused to give her money and ordered servants to take orders from him only. She lost a great deal of weight, unable to eat unless Stoney allowed her to, and often wore worse clothes than the servants. He invited guests, including his numerous mistresses, to the house and ordered her to act oddly in front of them, either answering only yes or no, or to comment on the weather or, sometimes, to refuse to speak at all, leading to doubts about her sanity. He forbade her to pursue any of her interests, prevented her from writing, he destroyed her gardens, and on one occasion made her destroy the plants herself. He even masterminded a plot to obtain custody of Mary Eleanor's two daughters by the Earl of Strathmore. On this rare occasion he was defeated, by the indomitable Lady Maria Jane, who refused to go with him but he was successful with Lady Anna Maria, whom he may even have seduced. When Stoney wrote a letter threatening to send Mary Eleanor to an asylum, she gave it to Lady Anna for safekeeping but she destroyed it. Stoney controlled every person in the household, even raping some of the servants. In the words of his friend and co-conspirator, Jesse Foot, 'the Countess from henceforth may truly be pronounced to be dead alive'.[72]

Mary Eleanor's chance to escape finally came after eight years, with the arrival of a maid named Mary Morgan. At the time, Stoney was making threats to kill Mary Eleanor and had started constructing an alibi, spreading rumours that she was about to die of a broken heart because she did not have access to the children of her first marriage. Mary, however, saw the evidence of physical abuse. Most notably, she had to assist when Stoney clawed at Mary Eleanor's skin so violently that it took two handkerchiefs and a towel to soak up the blood and halt the bleeding. After these years of mental and physical torture, she was a complete wreck. Foot would later say that her 'mind and body jointly submitted to receive the pressure which [Stoney], like a mangle, daily rolled upon them, and both were grievously collapsed.'

Mary Morgan encouraged Mary Eleanor to confide in her. The two formed a genuine friendship, and they were later joined by other sympathetic maids, Ann Parkes and Ann Dixon.

She was also strengthened by the arrival of old friends who were willing to assist her to escape from Stoney. Apprehensive that Mary Eleanor might one day sue him for separation, Stoney re-employed many old servants whom he had previously sacked, either because they had been Mary Eleanor's servants before their marriage, or because they had smuggled food to her against his orders. By doing so, he could maintain control over the servants and prevent them from being called to give evidence against him. One was footman George Walker, who had carried letters to her lover of long ago, James Graham, during her first marriage. She had trusted him so much that she had given him a copy of the pre-nuptial deed confirming her sole control over her income. Learning that he still possessed the deed, Mary Eleanor began to form a plan with the help of Mary Morgan, sending her out to consult a barrister, who confirmed that she would be eligible for legal protection should she leave the marital home.

On 3 February 1785, all seemed normal. A footman was despatched to collect a book for the Countess. Mary Morgan happily chatted away to the housekeeper about the latest bonnets. Ann Parkes picked an argument with one of the footmen, providing some entertainment for those below stairs. And Mary Eleanor sneaked out of the house in clothing borrowed from a servant. A woman born into the upper classes was escaping her marital prison only by the assistance of those considered beneath her, and who had very little in the world. She had locked the doors in order to try and prevent her escape being discovered for as long as possible but she had only just left when she saw Stoney racing back towards the house, searching for a glimpse of her. Luckily, she was not discovered and she took up residence in Dyers Buildings in Holborn with her loyal maids, who had left the house directly after her escape. She was now living on the charity of her social inferiors.

Society did not understand her actions, duped by Stoney's outward charm and well-planned propaganda campaign. Immediately, despite her lack of funds, Mary Eleanor launched three legal cases in order to secure her freedom from her dastardly husband. On the basis of her maids' testimony, she obtained an order that Stoney be bound over to keep the peace for 12 months, and she was protected by a court constable, who guarded her in her new home. In theory this should have kept her safe while her other cases, for ecclesiastical and legal separation, were heard in the courts.

While these progressed, Stoney launched an attack against the separation. Firstly, he sent out detectives to find Mary Eleanor. While he did so, he launched a public relations campaign, publicly stating that he would not force her to return and suggesting terms for a separation agreement which he would be legally bound to follow, projecting an image of a reasonable man. He also hid witnesses who could testify against him, such as Dorothy Stephenson, a former maid whom Stoney had repeatedly raped, then left pregnant and imprisoned in a brothel so that she could not speak out against him. Mary Eleanor's chances of success rested mainly on the prenuptial deed that Stoney was convinced no longer existed. Fortunately for Mary Eleanor, George Walker delivered his copy to her before Stoney searched his belongings. More assistance came from tenants at her estates, who sent her produce so that she and her maids would not starve, and sent her their rent money instead of Stoney. This enabled Mary Eleanor to search for witnesses of Stoney's cruelty, who could confirm her story. Her cause was aided when Stoney was forced to give up Dorothy Stephenson to the King's Bench and return her to her parents. Her account of rape, abduction, imprisonment and abuse swayed even more tenants to Mary Eleanor's side. However, the vast majority of society, still influenced by Stoney's propaganda and by Mary Eleanor's previous scandalous affair, remained distanced from her.

Stoney grew infuriated as he saw control slipping away from him. He redoubled his efforts to find Mary Eleanor and tormented tenants whom he discovered helping her. Desperate, he even sponsored pornographic cartoons slandering Mary Eleanor. Escaping from him a second time, after he located her lodgings, Mary Eleanor launched her own campaign, distributing posters around her Durham estate stating that she would endure 'dangers, still greater, if possible, than those to which I have hitherto been exposed' and 'starve in the most miserable manner' before she returned to Stoney. She was, unfortunately, to be held to this.

On 10 November 1786, Mary Eleanor was travelling down Oxford Street with her new admirer, Captain Farrer, and her saviour, Mary Morgan, when she realised that her carriage had been overtaken. The bodyguard that the court had provided had been bribed to hand her over, and criminals employed by Stoney had taken over the carriage. Mary slipped away in order to raise the alarm while Captain Farrer was thrown out of the coach. They were unable to stop Mary Eleanor from screaming out of the window all the way to Highgate, where Stoney entered the carriage at the Red Lion. His purpose was either to force her to abandon the separation or to cohabit with him, which would have invalidated everything he had done until that point.

She never stopped trying to escape as they continued north. When they changed horses at Barnet, she smashed the carriage window and cried out: 'Murder, for God's sake help me!' At another stop, having been told they were heading towards St Paul's Walden Bury in Hertfordshire, she wrote a note to Mary Morgan telling her where she could be found and asking for help. In Cambridgeshire, she asked a maid to send a messenger to Lord Mansfield, to request his assistance. Even though she was so distressed that she vomited, the maid conveniently believed Stoney's assurances that she was ill because she had been fasting, and the message was never sent. At Stilton, she was held at gunpoint while Stoney tried to force her to withdraw the separation. When she refused, he punched her in the head. She escaped and made it out of the inn and up the High Street but people refused to come to her aid and Stoney captured her again.

Further attempts to seek help all failed until they reached Nottinghamshire, where she managed to tell a maid that she had been abducted and make her agree to send a message to the courts in London. All her efforts were to no avail, however, and she was taken to her ancient family seat of Streatlam Castle in County Durham. When she reached the castle, she was held at gunpoint, repeatedly beaten and threatened with rape while she refused to sign the documents withdrawing all her legal cases against her husband. At one point, the trigger was actually pulled but the gunpower did not ignite.

While this was taking place, Mary Morgan was travelling round London with Mary Eleanor's lawer, Thomas Lacey, in an attempt to gain help. In an era before an organised police force, she had to wait a full day before legal notices were served. There was momentary elation when Mary Eleanor's note appeared, saying she was being taken to St Paul's Walden Bury but this soon turned to despair when they found she was not there. Bills were distributed throughout the capital asking people to 'use their utmost Endeavours to stop their progress, wherever they go, and prevent her being conveyed out of the Kingdom, and give every possible and speedy information thereof'. As reports came in of Mary Eleanor's reluctant progress north, forces were summoned from around the country to help track Mary Eleanor and return her to safety. Tenants from her estates volunteered their services, and her eldest son left Cambridge 'determined to liberate his mother out of her present disagreeable situation at the risk of his existence'. Word had spread of Mary Eleanor's presence at Streatlam, and miners had surrounded the castle, lighting large bonfires to announce their presence. When magistrates issued a warrant demanding that she should be set free, lawyers burst into the castle with a team of local supporters, tripping over a copy of the warrant ordering Mary Eleanor to be set free which had been left lying in the hall, and proceeded to search the place.

Stoney had, however, removed Mary Eleanor from the castle four days before. While her supporters were searching Streatlam, she was trekking over the Pennines with Stoney and one of his endless stream of pregnant mistresses. Mary Eleanor, exhausted both physically and psychologically, coped by telling Stoney her plans for the future once she had escaped him. Locals who saw them were amazed that the two women had survived the ordeal. Their progress was eventually thwarted, partly because the inns along the way recognised the group and refused to assist them, being fearful of legal repercussions and partly because the poor weather made it impossible for them to continue.

Descriptions of the group, in slightly unflattering terms, had been circulated around the North East region. Stoney was described as having a 'large nose which stands rather one side' and as being 'above the middle size', while Mary Eleanor was described as 'bulky'. They enabled a ploughman named Gabriel Thomas to recognise Mary Eleanor. He requested assistance from the parish constable, and by the time he caught up with the exhausted group, the rescuers numbered

12. They must have been brave men because they refused to leave Mary Eleanor, even though they were unarmed and Stoney threatened to shoot them. Rather than allow Mary Eleanor to go free, one of her captors attacked her with a sword but she successfully disarmed her assailant by pinching his arm. In the confusion, the constable grabbed Stoney's pistols and hit him over the head, knocking him off his horse and leaving him dazed and defenceless on the ground. By this point, Mary Eleanor had climbed onto a horse and exclaimed triumphantly: 'Farewell, learn to amend your life!' She turned her horse around and headed straight for London, where she arrived 24 hours later.

This dramatic interlude was the worst mistake that Stoney could have made. The public facade he had maintained for so many years was destroyed. Reports of her forcible abduction were to spread as far as India, and observers were shocked to see how exhausted Mary Eleanor was from her ordeal, having to be carried into court. The *Public Advertiser* wrote that she had 'experienced the greatest hardships and distress... almost too dreadful to relate'. The *English Chronicle* reported that 'Lady Strathmore, from the extreme ill-treatment she has received since forced from this metropolis, is become an object of the most extreme pity and compassion to every beholder'. Pamphlets and poems flooded the capital, recounting Mary Eleanor's abduction by her villainous husband and the dramatic tale of her heroic rescue. Stoney continued to try and regain control over the situation, but by now his tales were so ridiculous that, although they provided salacious gossip, they did not stand up in court.

Eight months after the abduction, Andrew Stoney was fined £300 and sentenced to three years' imprisonment. The heaviest blow, however, was that he would have to seek out guarantors prepared to find a total sum of £20,000 before he could be released. Further victories occurred when the Court of Chancery ruled that Mary Eleanor's pre-nuptial deed giving her complete control over her income was valid. For the first time since her marriage to Stoney 11 years earlier, Mary Eleanor was financially secure. Two years after this, the last of Mary Eleanor's legal cases, suing for a separation, was finally heard. Stoney fought on to the end, alleging that the now numerous witnesses to his cruelty and adultery had been bribed but his reputation preceded him. It took the jury just half an hour to grant Mary Eleanor her freedom. When the news reached the tenants on her estates, they rang the church bells in jubilation. When Mary Eleanor settled the bulk of her fortune on her eldest son and out of Stoney's reach – her former husband retaining only an annual allowance – Stoney relinquished both the children born during their marriage to Mary Eleanor's custody. Once they could bring him no financial gain he had no use for them. She had her children, her money and the companionship of the servants who had helped her. Mary Eleanor was free.

The legal system, however, did not always help abused wives. Twelve years after the death of Mary Eleanor Bowes in 1812, another woman made her marriage vows in a most 'happy state of mind' which would all too quickly evaporate. Like many, Lady Emily Cecil would attempt to use legal methods to protect herself, but despite her evident gumption and determination, she would fail disastrously. The marriage of George Nugent, Marquess of Westmeath and Lady Emily Cecil was supposedly a love match. Later, once the marriage had disintegrated, the couple would quibble as to whom had chased whom, and how many times Lord Westmeath had proposed before Lady Emily had accepted, but before their marriage there were references by acquaintances to the couple being 'very much in love'. Later, the Marquess would refer to his letters as the 'stupid recitals of a man very much in love with his own wife'.[73] It was not a particularly glittering match for Lady Emily; Lord Westmeath's parents had been divorced in 1796, and it was common knowledge that he had an illegitimate child. Despite their title, the Nugent family estates were heavily in debt and Lord Westmeath would later complain that the expenditure necessary to maintain Lady Emily in the style to which she was accustomed 'compromised' him economically.

Despite the seemingly positive beginning, the marriage was already experiencing severe problems by the birth of their first child, Lady Rosa. Family harmony was non-existent. Lady Westmeath would later allege that her mother-in-law had advised her to have an affair with a close friend, the Duke of Wellington, in order to advance Lord Westmeath's career, saying, 'if you would make use of your prettiness as other women do, you might put [your husband] at the top of the tree'. Later, once the marriage had completely dissolved, Lord Westmeath denied this, but during reconciliation attempts he admitted that his mother had 'acted most unjustifiably by you'. Sex was also problematic. Lady Emily would complain that he had given her erotic books to read, asked her to pose naked, and used indecent contraceptive practices, while he retaliated by claiming that she had cut off sexual relations altogether. Furthermore, he had told Lady Emily's brother, Viscount Cranbourne, to inform her that he had a child by a woman whom he had seen a few times, which she had accepted.

This, however, was only half the truth. In reality, the lady in question was a long-standing mistress by whom he had had two children, and he had no intention of relinquishing her. Not only was there inevitable jealousy to contend with but Lady Emily was upset that he was giving them 'a considerable part of his income' at a time when the Westmeaths were strapped for cash. Although the couple reconciled and Lord Westmeath agreed to stop seeing his mistress, Lady Emily still feared that the marriage would break down permanently. She wrote, 'it will depend entirely upon yourself whether we are for the future to live peaceably and happy together... if you do not entirely get rid of the whole of that infamous gang, your good sense must tell you it is impossible for us to live together without making ourselves miserable. If I were indifferent, you might have your objects and engagements separate from mine; but as you know well that I have no other object in the world than you, I cannot endure such want of sincerity... I must have all or nothing'.[74]

The principal reason that the marriage was in danger of collapsing was that Lord Westmeath had become physically abusive and would frequently lose his temper. On one occasion he was imprisoned for three months for provoking others to fight, and on another, had to be physically restrained from attacking the Lord Chancellor. Lady Westmeath's maid, Sarah MacKenzie, would later describe him as 'more like a madman than a reasonable being'. Witnesses confirmed

95

that Lady Westmeath was frequently beaten and that she would call out for assistance in the middle of the night. They described occasions of savagery, when she was forced to lock her husband out of the bedroom in self-defence. Although he would promise not to beat her if she opened the door, he would resume hitting her as soon as she did. At least once he tried to smother her with a pillow. Even when she was eight months pregnant, he kicked her in the side while he beat her.

Two years later, during their first separation, Lady Westmeath wrote, 'when my child was 12 hours in the world, you told me you would be damned if you gave 25 guineas a year to a bitch of a nurse... three weeks after the child was to be disinherited'. Lord Westmeath did not deny any of these accusations. On the contrary, he added that he had also threatened to throw both mother and child out of the house, and that he had intentionally lied to her about his future income.

Under these circumstances, it is not surprising that Lady Emily left her husband, taking her three-year-old daughter with her, and prepared to sue him for separation on the grounds of cruelty. He wrote her a series of impassioned letters during the separation, accepting blame for the marital breakdown and describing the 'brutality I have shown you. When I look back on the principal part of my conduct, it was that of a person totally unworthy... if you have been intemperate my folly and unworthiness have driven you to it... May God bless and comfort you for the blast I have made of your happiness'. The couple reconciled on this occasion, partly because Lady Emily's mother, Lady Salisbury, had begged her on her knees 'not to make themselves the talk of the town', promising her a home if he ever attacked her again and also because Lord Westmeath had agreed to sign a new financial settlement. He demonstrated that he would provide both mother and child with financial security, saying that he: 'shall never be at rest until that Settlement is executed... My soul is on the rack to think that you have been brought into money distress... by my selfishness'.[75] The settlement prevented Lord Westmeath from carrying out his previous threats of disinheritance. Not only did her daughter Lady Rosa inherit most of her mother's own money but, in addition, the vast majority of her father's estates. This was an extremely unusual move, as ancestral

A humorous
depiction of a
witness being
examined
during a trial
for adultery in
1818.

Cross examination of a witness in a case of Crim Con.

(*Above*) 'High Life at Noon': This 1769 series of images shows how popular adultery was supposed to be in high society. A man propositions a servant, while another woman receives a letter from her lover.

(*Middle*) 'High Life at Midnight': A woman takes advantage of a robbery to escape her lover's room without being noticed, but is then accidentally doused with the contents of a chamber pot.

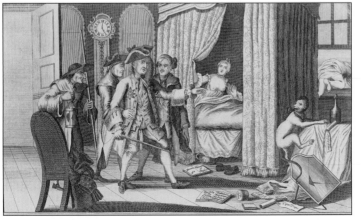

'High Life at Five in the Morning': A duke arrives home drunk to find his wife in bed with her lover. He draws his sword but the man has already escaped through the window.

'The Danger of Crim Con': A man rejects his lover's advances as he is unable to afford to pay her husband damages for taking his wife in adultery.

This image compares two stereotypes of late eighteenth century husbands. One husband prepares to strike his wife with a stick, while another husband cowers before his domineering wife.

'A Contented Cuckold in the New Fashion': This 1680 engraving shows a man counting the wealth that he has gained from his wife's adultery. This image shows that increased discussion was taking place on female adultery.

'A poor man loaded with mischief, or matrimony, drawn by Experience, engrav'd by Sorrow': Some found it difficult to escape an unhappy marriage. This man, depicted in 1752, is chained to wedlock, carrying the great burden of his drunken, unfaithful wife on his back.

The PLEASURES of the MARRIED STATE.

A Wife so chaste, so tender, and so kind,   Are blessed Guardians 'gainst all human woes,
So lovely in her Person, and her mind;   Unknown to idle Rakes, to Fops, and Beaus;
The gentle smiling Girl, the pratling Boy,   These are the Pleasures of the Social State,
The Fathers comfort, and the Mothers joy: View this you Batchelors, & mourn your fate.

London, Printed for Rob.t Sayer in Fleet Street, & Jn.o Smith in Cheapside.

'The Pleasures of the Married State': a rare depiction of a happy marriage.

(*Above*) George IV rages against those who refuse to support his proposed divorce from his wife Queen Caroline. (*Below*) The House of Lords is set up for a divorce trial. This particular trial is that of Queen Caroline, wife of George IV.

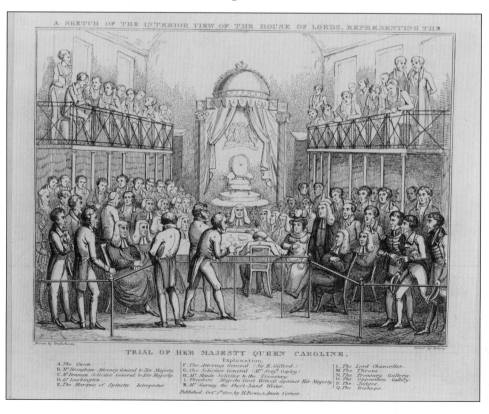

A wife discovers her husband making love with a servant and rages against her, saying 'Get out of my house, you hussey, I hired you to do your own business, not mine'.

A nineteenth century lord discovers to his horror that his wife has been publically ridiculed as an adulteress.

'A Receipt for Courtship': A wealthy man respectfully courts a woman of the same social class in 1805.

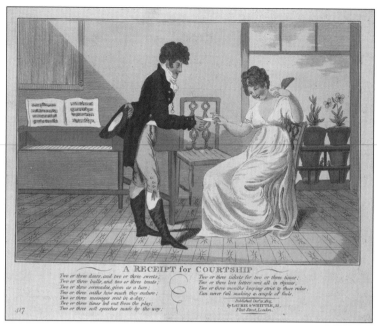

'The Whim': A more common view of marriage. A rake sitting in a tavern says, 'If ever I marry a wife, I'll marry a landlord's daughter, Then I can sit in the bar, And drink cold brandy & water'.

estates held in conjunction with an aristocratic title were almost always entailed towards the male line. He also gave up the administration of his estates to Lady Emily, taking only a personal allowance. Simultaneously, Lord Westmeath signed a prospective deed of marital separation, which guaranteed Lady Emily an allowance and full custody of their daughter.

The fact that Lord Westmeath granted Lady Westmeath full custody of their child when the law automatically granted custody to the father, shocked lawyers of the time. William Sheldon, the Cecil family lawyer, would later tell Lord Westmeath that he would rather have cut off his hand than sign such a deed. Yet the deeds were only a temporary improvement. Lady Westmeath became pregnant again but by the time she was two months pregnant the couple had stopped cohabiting, this time forever. Again, Lady Emily wanted to sue for separation but was dissuaded by her mother and legal advisers. Instead, she drew up a second separation deed, giving her full custody of both the children and a very generous allowance of £1,800 a year. Lord Westmeath was not to sue for the restitution of conjugal rights and he was to allow her to live wherever and with whomever she pleased. He needed some convincing to sign this deed – he tore up one copy in a fit of anger when he heard that Lady Emily was boasting about her triumph – but he did so eventually. Bizarrely, however, when she moved into her own London townhouse, she did so with her husband, as her mother and the family lawyer had convinced her to conceal the failure of the marriage from the world at large. The couple occupied the same house but had separate bedrooms, while her maid stood guard to prevent Lord Westmeath from attempting to enforce his marital rights.

Later events indicate that he saw this as a temporary situation which he only needed to tolerate until Lady Emily calmed down. She, however, viewed the separation as permanent. When they still had not reconciled in 1819, a year after their final separation agreement was signed, Lord Westmeath tried to persuade her to destroy the separation deeds and to reconcile with him, using the Duke of Wellington as an intermediary. These negotiations broke down when he quarrelled with the Duke and challenged him to a duel. The duel was narrowly avoided but he forbade the Duke to have contact with Lady Emily. The next time the Duke came to visit, Lord Westmeath threw him out of the house and began dismissing the servants, breaking into Lady Emily's belongings and going through her private financial papers. He refused to stop, screaming: 'I will have no more of these separate doings, I will be master in my own house'.[76] Lady Emily left the house with her children: the marriage had now openly broken down.

Around this time, Lord Westmeath accepted that his marriage was at an end and set about trying to find evidence that Lady Emily was having an affair with the Duke of Wellington in order to obtain a parliamentary divorce. It is unclear whether he genuinely believed this, or whether their frequent meetings provided him with a convenient excuse. His capacity for self-denial was so great that he may have convinced himself that an affair was the only reason that Lady Emily would refuse to reconcile with him.

Lady Westmeath was soon forced to relinquish both her children, even her six-month-old baby, when it was decided that a man could not legally sign away his rights to his children under Georgian law. She described this as a 'misfortune as makes me nearly unmindful of all the rest'. Once Lord Westmeath had the children in his care, he placed the house under watch and bribed the nursemaid to notify him if ever the Duke came to visit. This plot failed to work, partly because it was found out in its early stages and the nursemaid dismissed, and also because Lady Westmeath now never met the Duke without both her brother and a solicitor present. Lord Westmeath, however, continued to spread rumours that a divorce would soon occur, with the result that in 1823 a newspaper reported that a lawsuit by Lord Westmeath against Lady Westmeath for her adultery was imminent.

Further distress came when the Westmeaths' infant son died from hydrocephalus a few months after he was removed from her care, and Lady Rosa was given up to the Duke of Buckingham, who acted as her guardian. From this moment, all contact between mother and daughter was forbidden. It must have hurt Lady Westmeath that her husband had gone to such lengths to remove Lady Rosa from her custody, only to give her up. She occasionally managed to smuggle letters to Lady Rosa in a laundry basket. On one occasion in 1825 she stormed into Buckingham House (now Buckingham Palace), where Lady Rosa was staying, and was forcibly thrown out. In the same year, she broke into the house of Rosa's dancing teacher and locked Rosa and herself in a room upstairs while she tried to persuade her to leave with her. By this time, however, both Lord Westmeath and the Duke of Buckingham had impressed upon her that she should not go anywhere with Lady Emily, and she burst out in between sobs: 'Papa and the Duke of Buckingham have pointed out to me what sort of woman you was. I never wish to see your face again'. As far as can be known, they never communicated again until Lady Rosa became engaged to Fulke Greville 15 years later.

With one child dead and another estranged, Lady Emily had little else to do other than pursue her own rights in the courts. Two cases were heard simultaneously, spanning 17 separate lawsuits. One was in the equity and common-law courts, which aimed to enforce the maintenance allowance agreed to in the separation deeds. Another was a lawsuit in the ecclesiastical court, where Emily sought a separation on the grounds of cruelty and adultery and George counter-sued for a restitution of conjugal rights, where marital cohabitation would be restored. The first case would last for 11 years, ending in 1831, the second dragging on for 13 years until 1834.

Lord Westmeath's lawyers began their attack by claiming that all private separation deeds should be considered invalid. This did not work and Lady Westmeath successfully sued for the payment of her separation allowance. When he refused to comply, bailiffs in Ireland somewhat unfairly seized the cattle of 500 of Lord Westmeath's tenants to pay for Lady Emily's maintenance. Lord Westmeath boarded up his windows, and locked and barred the gates to stop his own goods being seized, giving orders that if any person tried to break into the property they were to be shot. He invented fictitious debts against his property in order to stop Lady Emily claiming it and encouraged his tenants to resist the bailiffs 'and to treat them like robbers', pulling legal strings to stop them being punished when they were prosecuted.

By doing so, he was successful in protecting the vast majority of his property.[77]

Lady Westmeath retaliated by encouraging her creditors to sue him for her debts. When they succeeded, he was imprisoned for four months. Until this point, Lady Emily had been remarkably successful by the standards of her day – she had had her very large allowance upheld by the court and when it had not been paid, had taken steps to have it enforced, and had Lord Westmeath imprisoned. This luck, however, was not to last.

This last lawsuit encouraged Lord Westmeath's lawyers to raise the question of whether the couple had actually been separated before Lady Emily left the family home in 1819. If a separation was followed by a period of reconciliation and cohabitation, any separation deeds were judged to be invalid. Lady Westmeath's lawyers argued, correctly, that there had been no reconciliation. They had not been sleeping together and Lord Westmeath had had no jurisdiction over the house. Lord Westmeath's lawyers pointed out, again correctly, that in the eyes of society, they had been a happily married couple. Only the servants knew the true state of the marriage.

Eventually, the judges decided that sharing the same home did count as a reconciliation, a decision confirmed by the House of Lords in 1827. As such, the separation deed was worthless and Lord Westmeath was only obliged to give his wife the pocket money she had received during their marriage. The secrecy Lady Salisbury had urged upon the couple, against Lady Emily's wishes, had destroyed her plan and all her efforts to protect herself legally. The failure of her long and expensive 12-year battle devastated her, leaving her embittered against her own family.

This ruling affected Lady Emily's battle to obtain a legal separation through the ecclesiastical courts as well. Although the episodes of cruelty were well documented, most of her witnesses were servants. Lord Westmeath, on the other hand, had influential witnesses such as the Countess of Glengall, Lord Arthur Hill and, most destructively, Lady Westmeath's own mother. Lady Westmeath's case was severely damaged by a lack of family support. Her brother, Viscount

Cranbourne, was named as one of her trustees but he was open to compromise and cautioned her against quarrelling with newspapers that printed libellous information. This was sound advice but it led to her breaking off their relationship. Another relative named as a trustee, Lord Talbot, utterly refused to act for her.

Most damagingly, her mother testified that Lord Westmeath 'never... treated his wife with cruelty or harshness or quarrelled with her or behaved to her with violence or treated her with coarse or insulting language', and described her daughter as 'not kind'. Lady Salisbury's refusal to support her daughter meant that she could not convincingly contradict Lord Westmeath's claims that Lady Westmeath had never 'put herself under the protection of her family'. It is difficult to explain Lady Salisbury's actions. Lady Emily would later say that Lord Westmeath had threatened to expose details of their private lives 'before the public'. Her earlier preoccupation with discretion and concealing scandal at all costs makes this plausible. Relations finally came to an end when Lady Salisbury refused a judge's request to take care of Lady Rosa temporarily until the case was resolved, saying: 'I will keep no children from their father'. Lady Salisbury later wrote, 'I will not expose myself anymore to the insolence of a daughter who ought to have better feelings, and who chooses to prefer others to her natural advisers', and they remained estranged until her death.

Other witnesses later testified that Lady Emily was a bully. A friend said that 'her ladyship has always succeeded in getting what she wished from him by bullying', while a servant remarked that Lord Westmeath seemed afraid of her.[78] While this may have been so to all outward appearances, he was clearly not too afraid to attack her brutally. Lord Westmeath was a disingenuous character. His refusal to accept any responsibility for the breakdown of the marriage, blaming Emily and a cast of other assorted characters throughout the years, demonstrates how difficult he must have been to live with.

Another obstacle was their earlier fake reconciliation and cohabitation. This meant that Lord Westmeath's lawyers could argue that she had accepted and forgiven his cruelty, making it legally useless. Lady Emily therefore needed more recent claims to bolster her case. She could not provide evidence of further cruelty when they had not seen each other for three years, so she began to accuse her husband of adultery. It seems unlikely that Lord Westmeath had suddenly ceased having extramarital relationships after having multiple affairs throughout his marriage. Lady Westmeath, however, had no reliable evidence for this, so she started to search for witnesses. This was not unusual. People spent vast amounts of money on finding, bribing and coaching witnesses in marital separation cases, the Westmeaths being no exception.

Eventually, a man named John Monaghan appeared, claiming that he could produce one of Lord Westmeath's mistresses, a written sexual contract between them, also two of their children, registered with the surname of Nugent. The evidence suggests that Lady Westmeath truly believed that Monaghan and the supposed mistress, Anne O'Connell, were genuine. Her delight in eventually finding a witness echoes across the years. 'Believe me when I say that I never would ask or bribe any person, much less such a man as you, to tell me an untruth,' she wrote, adding, 'I *never forget a kindness*... You have come forward voluntarily to assist a much injured person, and as long as I live I shall never forget it'.[79]

Such happiness at finding a witness at last suggests that Lady Westmeath was not fabricating evidence; if so, she could easily have done so long before this. The claims, however, were false. Anne O'Connell could not produce the contract, the children, or indeed any evidence of their existence. She claimed she could not even remember their names. At this point, Lady Emily should have abandoned the witness but either determination or desperation made her push on, and she had them brought to England and placed in a safe house so that Lord Westmeath could not retrieve them. Lord Westmeath tried to use this as evidence to suggest that Lady Emily had deliberately set out to deceive the court but this was standard behaviour in a legal case. Despite the fact that she was blatantly lying, the evidence of Anne O'Connell should have been enough to obtain a legal separation. Anne, however, was badly prepared. Lady Emily may have been desperate to believe that she was a genuine witness but her legal team should still have primed her. When Anne O'Connell took the stand, she could not describe any of the rooms at Clonyn, Lord Westmeath's house, or even the route from her house to Clonyn, claiming that she was always drunk. She also admitted that Lady Emily had promised her a post in her household worth £30. Other witnesses made similarly poor showings and admitted that they had been given money and promised positions in order to testify. Yet again, Lady Emily had been terribly let down. She narrowly avoided being convicted of conspiracy to frame, and her case for cruelty and adultery was rejected. In 1826, seven years after she left her husband for good, she was ordered to return to him, which was a devastating setback.

But Lady Emily did not give up. Her appeal to a higher court was heard a year later. Wading through the 'immense mass of evidence', the judge, Sir John Nicoll, came to two significant conclusions. Describing cruelty in aristocratic marriages as 'far more severe and insupportable' than in working class marriages, he made two important declarations: that the Westmeaths had not reconciled in 1818, and that George was so 'domineering and despotic' before their final separation that earlier evidence of his cruelty was admissible. He declared that 'Lady Westmeath has sufficiently proved her first allegation, charging her husband with cruelty, and is, on that account, entitled to a sentence of separation'. Emily was granted her freedom and George was ordered to pay her alimony of £700 a year and her legal costs.

Despite this major victory, the legal wrangling continued. For the next two years, until 1829, Lord Westmeath made various attempts to appeal against this judgement. They came to nothing but he still used a wide variety of creative legal strategies to avoid paying both Lady Emily's legal costs and her alimony. Even worse, in 1834 he eventually managed to have Lady Westmeath's alimony reduced to just £300 a year (under £15,000 in today's money). This was drastically reduced from the maintenance he had agreed to pay her 11 years earlier when she first negotiated her ground-breaking legal agreement. Portions of her legal costs had still not been paid as late as 1853. They were both also heavily in debt due to their long legal battle. Lord Westmeath later estimated that he had spent at least £30,000 on his legal costs, equivalent to around £1.5 million today. Lady Emily ran into considerable trouble obtaining the portion of her inheritance because one of her trustees, Lord Talbot, refused to act for her. She faced an uphill battle for survival, and she had to resort to exploiting her personal connections.

In 1818 she was appointed as a Lady-in-Waiting to Princess Adelaide, Duchess of Clarence, wife of the future William IV. This not only gave her £250 a year but also free accommodation in St James's Palace. The Princess and Lady Westmeath formed a close personal friendship. The Clarences exerted themselves on several occasions for her, notifying her that newspapers were falsely reporting that she was about to be prosecuted for adultery. The Duke even wrote a letter to the Prime Minister, with whom he was not on good terms, asking that 'our excellent and ill-used friend, the Marchioness of Westmeath' be given a regular pension. Despite the fact that Lord Westmeath won the right to reduce alimony payments by the amount of this pension, Lady Westmeath still had a comfortable income of £1,850 a year, allowing her to make investments and live in a mansion in Piccadilly.

In 1839 she campaigned with Caroline Norton to help pass the Infant Custody Bill, which would overturn the principle that men had an automatic right to the custody of their children. In 1855, she published her own account of her marital legal battles, under the title *Narrative of the Case of the Marchioness of Westmeath,* which played a key role in influencing the passage of the 1857 Divorce Act.

Her personal life was miserable, however. She never rebuilt relations with her family. Her brother, Lord Salisbury, made several attempts at reconciliation but they were all rebuffed. She was convinced that he had worked with Lord Westmeath to derail her case. In her will, she would later write that her case was 'a warning to any woman placed in my painful and trying position. Let her avoid as a trustee a near relation or brother'.[80] She also rebuffed other relatives, such as Gerald Wellesley, who had testified in support of Lord

Westmeath's assertions that she was hot-headed, but her reply to his offer of reconciliation was, understandably, cold and detached, saying 'a renewal of our acquaintance in fact can only be distressing to both Parties and bring very melancholy recollection instantly to my mind'.[81] Lord Westmeath also made periodic attempts to provoke her, despite the fact that he had moved on with a mistress and child and was paying Lady Emily very little money. He succeeded in having his mistress listed as 'The Marchioness of Westmeath' in the *Court Circular* and when his illegitimate daughter died, inserted a notice in the newspapers referring to her as the 'Lady Mary Anne Nugent'. These actions, together with the fact that he continually called Emily by her maiden name, or the Dowager Marchioness of Westmeath, implied that they were divorced. As a divorce could only be obtained if a wife had been proven guilty of adultery, this was slanderous.

All this, however, paled in comparison to her estrangement from Rosa. At the time of Lady Rosa's engagement, Lady Westmeath wrote, 'I once idolised you, Rosa, and was more attached to you than I ought to have been to anything of this world'.[82] Lord Westmeath had spoken so negatively about Lady Emily, that Rosa's first letter in 14 years, in reply to her mother, was cold and hostile. Lady Westmeath was not clever enough to see that this letter could potentially have been the first step in forging a relationship with her daughter and friendly relations were not resumed. When she died, in January 1858, she was embittered and estranged, not only from her family but also the daughter for whom she had fought so hard.

In many ways Lady Westmeath had been a visionary, convincing her husband to sign a separation deed destroying the patriarchal privileges that society had given him, but through bad luck and poor advice, all her achievements were overturned. She herself seems to have believed that her life had been an unsuccessful one. Shortly before her death, she cut out a section from an unlabelled newspaper debating on the nature of success, which is still preserved among her papers today:

"I confess", says a thoughtful writer, "that increasing years bring with them an increasing respect for men who do not succeed in life, as those words are commonly used... I will not go so far as to say... that the world knows nothing of its greatest men; but there are forms of greatness, of at least of excellence, which die and make no sign, there are martyrs that miss the palm, but not the stake, heroes without the laurel, and conquerors without the triumph". [83]

CHAPTER 5

Parliamentary Divorces: Adultery on Stage

When Jane Austen writes in the closing chapter of *Mansfield Park* that 'Mr Rushworth has his divorce', she means that Mr Rushworth has used his exceptionally large income to obtain a Parliamentary Act terminating the marriage. Before 1858, a spouse – usually a husband – would petition the House of Lords to pass a Parliamentary Act which would dissolve their marriage 'as if the said Lady were dead'.[84] This allowed both husband and wife to remarry and move on with their lives. While this may sound straightforward, in reality public divorce proceedings, no matter how outwardly simple, were the result of a long and arduous process.

The divorce procedure before 1857 was a series of legal hoops that the petitioner (nearly always a man) had to jump through in order to get his divorce. Although the process was an uncertain one initially, by the late eighteenth century it started to take on a standardised form. The husband had first to secure a religious separation in a Church Court on the grounds of his wife's adultery, then sue his wife's lover for financial compensation in an action called 'criminal conversation'. Even after all this, before a divorce was granted, the Lords firstly had to see proof that: the wife had committed adultery, with a minimum of two witnesses willing to testify; secondly, that the marriage had been successful before the affair, with no prior evidence of neglect, cruelty or prior adultery by the husband; and thirdly, that the husband and wife had not colluded to provide evidence so that they could jointly end a marriage of which they had both tired.

Divorce records do not necessarily contain an accurate account of what actually happened. Think of the divorce court as a theatre where everybody wears a mask, everybody has their own agenda, and everybody will be presenting an artificially constructed version of events calculated to gain the sympathy of the Lords, and help them win. The 'betrayed' husband may in fact have a string of mistresses behind him. The ostensibly 'reluctant' wife may be secretly working together with her husband to help him free them both from a loveless marriage. The wife's lover may not be a lover at all but a friend pressed into service to provide the necessary evidence of adultery. Divorces were either the result of private negotiations between the husband and wife, or a sustained campaign by the husband to find enough proof to justify a divorce. This chapter will peel away the layers of artifice, lies and construction, to uncover the real lives, personalities and events that the rich of the day struggled so strenuously to conceal in their bids for divorce.

During the eighteenth century, the number of divorces expanded far beyond expectations. Divorces became so common that a churchman, Bishop Horsley, complained that 'divorce bills had been applied for and obtained, not merely by the higher ranks, but even by tradesmen and mechanics'.[85] While they had originally been set up as a way for the aristocracy to dispose of difficult wives and obtain a son to inherit their estates, ordinary people had proved that they were just as eager to get rid of their unwanted spouses. By 1800, only 18 per cent of divorcees were members of the aristocracy. Other petitioners came from much more humble backgrounds. Most of these were doctors and merchants, but there were also individuals such as butchers and piano makers. In 1700 Ralph Box, a druggist, obtained a divorce, as did Thomas Cobb, an engraver, in 1728; and a customs officer, Corbyn Morris, in 1746. In addition, and somewhat surprisingly, another sizeable group was the clergy.

The most important factor that gave people access to parliamentary divorces was not social status but money. Parliamentary divorces 'typically cost between £2-3,000, far beyond the means of ordinary folk'[86] and some could cost more than that, depending on how easily the bill was passed. To give us an idea of the scale, in 1800 this was equal to approximately £64,340 today and was the equivalent of the entire yearly income of Mr Bennet in *Pride and Prejudice*.

Witnesses who could supply the right evidence were absolutely crucial to a divorce's success, especially in the early days. Husbands primarily obtained proof of their wives' adultery through servants. In the houses of those rich enough to afford parliamentary divorces, servants would have observed every small detail of the lives of their rich employers. No matter how careful adulterous couples were, servants were always lurking in the wings. Unfaithful wives must have been petrified, not only that the servants would report to their masters, but also that they would gossip amongst themselves and that scandal would emerge that way.

Conversely, in a world where upper class lives depended upon the collaboration of servants, a trusted servant could also be used to assist the couple in their intrigues. Charlotte Calvert's personal maid, Mary Cockerell, used to let Johnson into the house and provide food to the couple in their bedroom. The fact that she was sacked as soon as Leonard Calvert found out about the liaison suggests that she was indeed a loyal servant to Charlotte.

Servants were the first to be questioned about their mistress's proclivities and often played a key role in the formation of divorce cases. Not only were they more susceptible to bribes due to their low wages, but they were more likely to find guarantees of permanent employment through the husband, who would often be the owner of a great estate, employing dozens of servants. People were keenly aware of the dangers and lack of privacy arising from observant servants. Exerting 'constant moral and sexual surveillance'[87] over their social superiors gave servants a certain power over their masters' lives, a fact they were not slow to appreciate. Some may have been genuinely upset that their betters were not following the expected moral codes. One servant who spotted her mistress's lover through a keyhole was not shy in crying out: 'You damned dog, what you do there?'[88] Leonard Calvert was alerted to his wife Charlotte's behaviour by a series of anonymous letters, which seem likely to have come from servants who were genuinely upset about the affair. He even managed to gather together a group of servants to chase her lover Tom Johnson off the property, eventually losing him in a cornfield.

Another reason that servants would have been preoccupied with their masters' lives was, quite simply, as a source of gossip to enlighten the dullness and monotony of domestic service. Charlotte Calvert's adulterous liaison became 'the daily discourse and table talk of the servants'.[89] The Duchess of Beaufort initially reacted with anger to reports that the servants were gossiping about her, saying: 'How durst the servants talk of me'[90] but then bursting into tears once she realised the power they had to ruin her.

Some servants might have accidentally come across evidence of adulterous liaisons, but it seems more likely that the majority deliberately set out to obtain some sort of proof that their superiors were up to no good. Charlotte Calvert's servants were 'deliberately on the watch'[91] for signs that her lover Tom Johnson was sneaking into the house. In 1798, Mrs Wilson's servant testified that he viewed her with her lover from 'outside of the house upon a ladder, which raised me as to look over the shutters of the window'. Similarly, one of Mrs Daly's maidservants hid behind a sofa in order to observe her embracing her lover, the Earl of Kerry. Many witnesses even made written memoranda, realising that an account of their mistress's adultery might one day prove valuable. Both John Pargiter and Robert Croucher, who spied on the Duchess of Beaufort and Lord Talbot on one of their escapades, wrote an account of what they had seen. When one witness was asked why he had taken the time to record what he had seen that day, he responded that 'he did not know but that some time or other he might be called upon to give an account of what he knew'.[92] What he really means is that he saw an opportunity to make money.

Servants could also team up in order to corroborate each other's stories and give them an added air of authenticity. Charlotte Calvert's nursemaid joined forces with another servant when spying on Charlotte, so that they could both confirm that they had heard a man's voice coming from Charlotte's bedroom. Temporary workers who would come in for the day and were not part of the household, could also be called as witnesses to provide additional proof. One of the servants, Mrs Carter, openly showed one visiting worker, an upholsterer, Charlotte's bed which displayed the imprint of two bodies. On other occasions, unconnected individuals would verify one another's stories, hoping that providing proof of an aristocrat's adultery would lead to financial gain. For example, the Duchess of Beaufort and Lord Talbot were observed by a farmer on one of their meetings. Although they had already been caught romping *al fresco* by a groom, they continued to meet outdoors. Not content to observe them by himself, however, the groom gathered a passing day labourer and a tailor to join him in following the couple, where they were discovered making love under the hedge. Aristocrats and the rich were under constant surveillance.

Servants could be quick to exploit potential blackmail opportunities. Servant surveillance could be a lucrative side business. This led to problems with wives who sought to hide their adultery from their husbands, as they clashed with servants eager to make their fortune. They were often exceedingly successful, extracting money and goods from both wives and lovers. For example, on the same day that the Duchess of Beaufort's assistant groom, John Pember, warned her of servant gossip surrounding her relationship with Lord Talbot, he was rewarded, firstly by the Duchess, who gave him ten guineas, and later by Lord Talbot, who gave him a further five-and-a-half-guineas. Although this may seem a small amount, 15 guineas was the equivalent of two years' income for an assistant groom. In addition, John was later promoted to the position of groom at double his previous wages, as well as being given two horses worth £40 (around £3,450 in today's money).[93] When such rich rewards were on offer to servants earning such low wages, it was not surprising that servants kept a 'keen lookout'[94] for any possible misbehaviour. Yet bizarrely, John appears to have left the money that he had made with the Duchess for safekeeping. Perhaps in this case he was so confident about her need for secrecy that he felt he could retrieve the money at any time.

Bribing a servant to keep quiet, was not always the easy dismissal that couples must have initially hoped it would be. John Pember continued to make demands on the Duchess of Beaufort in order to buy her silence. He refused to put in a full day's work (although with the workload expected of domestic servants in the eighteenth century, it is hard to blame him!) and demanded that the Duchess dismiss servants with whom he had quarrelled. When he was given warning to improve his behaviour, Pember flew into a rage, cautioning the Duchess via her butler that: 'I shall have an opportunity for telling her… for I know enough to blow her'.[95] If there had been any servants left in the Beaufort household who did not know of the Duchess's liaison after that outburst, there can hardly have been any left in ignorance. The Duchess was trapped and John Pember continued his employment in her household.

Husbands with money and resources were able to set up sinister surveillance systems through their servants in order to catch their wives (sometimes literally) in the act, providing enough evidence to get a divorce. This was the case with various aristocratic couples, the Duke and Duchess of Beaufort included. Once they had separated and the Duchess was installed in her own house in New Bond Street, the Duke started to lay a trap. He encouraged old servants whom he knew he could trust, to approach the Duchess and ask for employment. Several were told to keep a daily diary, to confirm that he had never stayed the night, so if the Duchess ever became pregnant, he could prove that it could not be his child.

The Duke of Grafton, Prime Minister of Great Britain from 1768 to 1770, took the same approach for his divorce, deploying a 'small army'[96] of detectives and spies to watch over his wife in 1768, while she was pregnant with her lover's child. The Duke adopted a two-pronged approach, employing outside watches and convincing existing servants, including the Duchess's personal maid, to give information. The Duke's agent, who oversaw the whole plot, was so worried that the Duchess might be similarly spying on the Duke that he took the somewhat paranoid move of writing his letters to the Duke in code.

From these letters, we can see how desperate the Duke was for evidence. The agent constantly reassures him about the scheme's likelihood of success, reporting triumphantly, 'it is scarcely possible that a doctor or midwife should have got into the house without the[ir] knowledge… or that there should be a live child'. He admits that a stillbirth would be more problematic, stating somewhat coldheartedly that, 'a dead child would be very unfortunate from the ease with which it might be concealed', but nevertheless, 'the persons who walk about the house are alert and will give intelligence of every person that goes in'.[97] The nooses were tightening around the necks of the two duchesses.

Other husbands were less subtle. Leonard Calvert obtained proof of his wife Charlotte's adultery by gaining entry to her house with the assistance of bailiffs and a gang of men. They did not have to break in, as one of her servants, who had presumably been bribed, let the group in. They broke open the lock on the bedroom door and rushed inside to find Charlotte and her current lover, Count Castelli, in bed together. Charlotte was stripped of all her jewels and possessions, and even the buckles from her shoes were removed. Afterwards, she was thrown out of her house with nothing except the clothes she was wearing. Perhaps the most unexpected part was that one of the men who worked with Leonard Calvert to trap Charlotte had worked for her since she was a child.[98] There was no mercy or loyalty when it came to adulterous wives in early modern England.

Women, therefore, found deciding where to meet their lovers problematic. Some wives, Charlotte Calvert for example, boldly smuggled their lovers into their bedrooms. Charlotte's nursemaid would testify that while spying on her employers, she caught Charlotte's lover, Tom Johnson, climbing into the family home through the drawing room window. Others attempted to hide their affairs by meeting in unusual places within the house. The first option was usually to seek out one of the communal rooms, such as a drawing room or dining room. These could be equally dangerous, however, as servants continually entered these rooms when their masters were not expected, to perform domestic duties such as cleaning or lighting fires. Locking the doors proved an equally tricky dilemma. On the one hand, it ensured that no one could enter the room but on the other, it could alert servants to the presence of illicit activities. It was difficult to avoid arousing servants' suspicions if visits lasted for several hours at a time and went on behind locked doors.

Adulterous couples would therefore meet in a series of increasingly unlikely places in their attempts to evade detection. Servants observed the Duchess of Beaufort and her lover, Lord Talbot, in a series of progressively more improbable locations. First, they were spotted in the Duchess's dressing room of her London townhouse, where the dishevelled Duchess was caught on the Baron's knee. Although she jumped up quickly, she was not fast enough to escape the servant's observation that the Duchess was unkempt and that her lover's trousers were unbuttoned. The Duchess then took the precaution of locking the door but this was simply an invitation for servants to listen at the keyhole, where they somewhat conveniently overheard the Duchess saying: 'You make me very hot. I am not able to bear it… I am afraid the servants suspect us'.[99] Further investigations revealed that the couple had constructed a makeshift bed by lining up dining room chairs, and items of the Duchess's clothing were found scattered around the room. They then started meeting outside, presumably because they thought they would be safer with just a groom to observe them rather than an army of housemaids and footmen. Sometimes they stayed in the carriage, while at other times they ran into the woods. Even there, however, they were not entirely safe. In a scene straight out of a comedy, the chaise burst open on one occasion to reveal the Duchess and Lord Talbot in the middle of making love.

Some couples would stage elaborate schemes to create opportunities to be alone. Charlotte Calvert and Tom Johnson organised riding expeditions across Oxfordshire with his wife and a married couple named Clements, making sure to cover such long distances that the party would need to stay the night at an inn. The fact that they constantly galloped off ahead of the party, often only to be found in the bedroom of a local inn, led to suspicions that the expeditions were not all they seemed. Soon, any pretence of respectability vanished when Mrs Johnson was suddenly removed from the party and Charlotte was exceptionally insistent that Mrs

Clements should continue to ride out with them, despite protests of illness. Furthermore, she was noted to be behaving oddly, refusing to share a room with Mrs Clements or to be locked in her room for safety, normal precautions for female travellers at this time. The final straw came when Mrs Clements found that Charlotte had additionally locked Mrs Clements into her room, leaving her no way of getting out, and the expeditions came to an end.

While servants had a great deal of power during their employer's marital discord, they could also be influenced and used by others – often the head of the household – to provide evidence. Records of the witnesses' testimonies provide little clues indicating that servants were often being directed by a skilful hand to provide the right kind of evidence. Some witness depositions read as if the witnesses had been prepared by professionals who wished to make absolutely sure that all the necessary and incriminating information was communicated to the House of Lords.

One example can be found in transcripts of witness testimonies in the divorce trial of Anne, Countess of Macclesfield in 1697. The Countess had lived apart from her husband for many years. Complaining that she had spoken of him with 'scorn and contempt', the Earl strongly declared that he would never live with her as long as he lived. Despite the fact that the Countess successfully exerted herself to save her husband when he was sentenced to death for being part of a plot to assassinate Charles II and his brother and heir, the Duke of York, he refused to consider cohabiting with her again.

Eventually she started a relationship with Earl Rivers, giving birth to two of his children. There was no chance of reconciliation and the Earl of Macclesfield had no legitimate children to inherit his estate. A divorce was necessary. The evidence suggests that he made sure that witnesses would provide ample and satisfactory testimony. For example, half-way through her maid, Dinah Allsop's, interrogation she suddenly burst out: 'I forgot to tell you that my Lady gave Mrs Richardson 20 Guineas'.[100] This term 'I forgot' makes it seem as though the witness came into court with a prepared statement. While this does not necessarily mean that the witness was lying – indeed the number and variety of independent witnesses in the Macclesfield case would indicate that she may very well have been genuine – it does indicate that there was some level of rehearsal before witnesses appeared in Parliament.

Witness selection was a tactical move on the battlefield that was the divorce court of the House of Lords. Lawyers specifically chose witnesses who appeared outwardly respectable and trustworthy. An examination of the numerous witness depositions given in the trial of the Duke and Duchess of Norfolk in 1700, for example, shows that the witnesses had several important characteristics in common. Firstly, approximately two thirds of them were married. Early courts went to considerable lengths to give great detail regarding the marital status of the witnesses. Margaret Elwood was described as having been 'married aboute 24 yeares', Jane Wadsworth is a 'wife', Thomas Lloyd is a widower and John Hall is a 'marryed man'.[101] Only two witnesses did not have their marital status disclosed. This high percentage is made even more remarkable when we consider that most servants would have been unmarried, so it seems likely that married servants were deliberately being chosen as witnesses. In a world where marriage meant status, respectability and independence, lawyers, probably rightly, thought that the evidence of married witnesses would carry more weight than the evidence of those who were single, regardless of what they had seen. Witnesses were clearly chosen on the basis of the impression they would make on the House of Lords.

Parliament was well aware that servants were vulnerable to bribery and manipulation by their employers. In a vain attempt to try and work out which witnesses could be trusted, the Lords initially tried to scrutinise them. During one of the very first divorces, that of the Earl and Countess of Macclesfield in 1697, witnesses were called to testify about the reputation and character of one of the key testators, Sarah Goochall. One of the witnesses called was Olive Mounteney, who was asked to give her opinion of Mrs Goochall, describing her as a 'juste woman'. William Banastre was asked to comment on her reputation and honesty, answering: 'She's a very honest woman... I don't think she would forswear herself'.[102]

Questioning could be more specific, focusing on the relationship between a servant and their mistress and whether any grudges or personal hostility existed between them. For example, a woman named Margaret Davis was asked to comment on whether one key witness in the Macclesfield case, Dinah Allsop, had any reason to lie about her mistress's behaviour.[103] These moves to investigate the credibility of witnesses disappear after the Macclesfield divorce and such intensive interrogation of both evidence and witnesses does not take place again. The rise in divorce cases once the first few cases were passed successfully, and the subsequent remarriages accepted as valid meant that it would have been impractical to subject every witness in a divorce case to such scrutiny, making it easier for witnesses bribed to lie or exaggerate, to escape the Lords' notice.

While in many ways men had the upper hand over their wives in divorce cases this was not the whole story. It was not as simple and as clear-cut as might first be expected. Their vulnerable, inferior position, the sexual double standards, and women's more limited economic power all suggest that women had little, if any, power over their everyday lives, much less a divorce on the public stage of the Houses of Parliament. Historians Crawford and Mendelson have gone so far as to say that 'the House of Lords was of the view that a man, irrespective of his own adultery, was entitled to divorce'.[104] Clever, resourceful and determined women, however, could and did find ways to thwart their husbands. There are examples of women not only assisting in their divorce cases, but in some cases, frustrating men's efforts entirely. It also fails to take into account that society expected certain standards of decency, honesty and fidelity from men as the 'superior sex'. If they failed to live up to these obligations, the court of public opinion could swiftly turn against them.

One of the ways in which women could frustrate men in divorce cases was the ability to refuse to assist or actively hinder the divorce efforts. Divorces were a much simpler affair if the husband could convince the wife to assist him by providing evidence of her own guilt. Before divorces could be granted on the basis of male adultery, the only way for a couple to divorce was by ensuring there was proof of the wife's adultery. If servants or spies proved ineffectual, the only way for a man to obtain a divorce was if the wife agreed to stage her own evidence by arranging to be caught in bed with a lover. The husband would usually convince the lover to go along with this arrangement by agreeing not to enforce any claims for the financial compensation he was entitled to as the result of a successful criminal conversation case. In 1769 the Duke of Grafton assured his wife's lover, the Earl of Ossory, that he would take 'no advantage of' the financial compensation awarded for his wife's adultery.

Although divorces were officially supposed to be rejected when collusion was indicated, not all were. In one 1783 case, a servant actually turned against both master and mistress to report that the master had been overheard saying to the accused lover: 'I have this one further favour to beg of you, Jack, that you will go to bed with Lady Maria and allow some of my servants to come in and see you in that situation, in order that I may obtain my divorce with as little trouble and expense as possible'. In this case, however, the servant was ignored. Only six divorce petitions were rejected between the years 1714-1779, even when it became obvious that there had been some degree of collaboration.[105] Evidence had to be absolutely undeniable in order to halt a divorce case.

One of the very rare occasions when a divorce case was halted due to evidence of collusion was the 1755 Moreau case. David Moreau had abandoned his wife Susannah many years before and had emigrated to Gibraltar. She had supported herself by going into service, before she started an affair with George Smedley. Susannah and her lover agreed to stage evidence for a divorce case, but the case collapsed when she produced a written agreement of collusion between herself, her husband and her mother-in-law, who was funding the case. Another signed contract was used in the divorce case of Thomas and Judith Edwards, where he agreed to provide her with £45 a year if she did not oppose the case in Parliament. Collusion was also proven in the 1778 case of Thomas Chism, a drysalter. He was ostensibly suing for divorce but it became obvious that his father-in-law, a gentleman of private means, was paying for the divorce, reputedly so that his daughter could marry someone of her own social class.[106] These cases, however, were few and far between.

Many women played an active role in their divorce cases. For example, Anne, Countess of Macclesfield, wrote her own petitions to Parliament asking them to delay her divorce case so that she could have time to transport her witnesses to London. Similarly, she asks for and is granted the opportunity to speak on her own behalf in the House of Lords, to defend herself against her brother-in-law, Fitton Gerrard.[107] Women were not necessarily mere passive recipients of their husbands' decisions and the courts' judgements.

One of the most striking episodes in which a wife most certainly held the upper hand over her husband was one of the earliest divorces, that of the Duke and Duchess of Norfolk in the 1690s. Mary, Duchess of Norfolk demonstrated how a wife could and did play a vital role in influencing the passage of a divorce bill. Firstly, she asked to be: 'Heard by your Lordships before such Bill be received'.[108] Her confidence is illustrated in one of her petitions to the House of Lords. Although she consistently followed the proper forms, she clearly felt that she was able to direct proceedings and influence the direction that questions would take. One letter states that the petitioner would 'rather humbly Insist that your Lordships would please to require the Duke to be particular and Certain in these Material Circumstances of his Charge'.[109] Clearly, confidence in the success of her endeavours could allow a wife to adopt a less subservient approach to the Lords.

The Duchess of Norfolk continued to manipulate the Lords cleverly through her letters, playing the role of the helpless woman, weak and unprotected. She complained to the House of Lords that her divorce proceedings were completely unexpected, saying: 'I find my prosecution to be now very violent'.[110] As she was protected by her own independent wealth, an army of powerful lawyers and her marriage had never been one of affection, this seems slightly disingenuous. She followed this with a letter stating that she 'never had or received from her Husband the last Intimation of any Misdemeanour on her Part against him, which Joynd to her Innocence... makes this proceeding before your Lordships very surprising to her'. Seeing as she was having a longstanding and well documented affair with Sir John Germaine, whom she would later marry after her divorce bill was passed, it cannot have been as surprising as she tried to claim.

She follows her portrayal of innocent female ignorance with clever requests which prove just how clearly the Duchess understood both her case and how she could fight back, asking to 'have a copy of the particular Charge against her with the Names of the Witnesses, And reasonable time allowed her to answer'.[111] This was the equivalent of a public announcement that she intended to fight the divorce every step of the way. Losing the title of Duchess meant that she would lose social prestige, rank and influence, which were important matters in the eighteenth century. Mary Norfolk was not going down quietly. She frustrated the Duke by poking holes in his legal case, which was not sufficiently supported by the standards of the time, writing that the charges were 'too general and is not pursuant',[112] an argument agreed with by the Lords. Her lover, Sir John, helped matters by paying for potential witnesses to be smuggled to Holland. When faced with such numerous obstacles, the Duke had to admit the defeat of his first divorce bill. The Duke only obtained his divorce when the Duchess stopped creating obstacles the following year. It is difficult to determine why Mary Norfolk changed her mind. Maybe she had decided that she wanted to marry her lover. Nevertheless, the Duchess of Norfolk proves that if a woman had money and brains, then she could hinder her divorce action significantly. Even after obtaining his divorce, the Duke was the loser in the end. He died barely a year after the bill had passed, having run out of time, unable to remarry and have the wife, heirs and children he had battled for, instead being succeeded by a nephew.

There are even cases where it is clear that women were initiating and guiding their own divorces. One of the most obvious examples is that of Mary Forester and Sir George Downing. Mary Forester's parents married her to Downing when she was just 13. The antipathy seems to have been instant and mutual. Although it would have been intended for them to cohabit once they were older, this never happened. Instead, Sir George took the opportunity to travel abroad for three years, declaring upon his return that he would never consummate the marriage or live with his wife. He seems to have objected to her taking up a position at Court, where she had achieved a considerable degree of success as Lady-in-Waiting to the Queen. The divorce petition did not mince words, referring to their mutual 'disgusts and aversions which have arisen and do continue', stressing that the marriage only took place 'in obedience to your Petitioners parents, when they were of such tender years' and stressing that not only did they never live together but that Mary Forester had never changed her surname to Downing.

Although the dislike appears to have been reciprocal, the petition has clearly been initiated at the request of Mary Forester, who describes how she is 'desirous of being released from her unhappy engagement'. Despite the fact that George Downing co-signs the petition, it was written by Mary Forester's lawyers, from her perspective and upon information supplied by her. Although the divorce was unsuccessful, as Mary Forester was unwilling to provide evidence of her own adultery, this does show that women prepared to do so could both possess and exercise the power to end their marriages.

The Countess of Anglesea was another woman who successfully sought redress through the courts in the 1690s. Although she did not petition for a divorce, she did petition the House of Lords for maintenance. It seems likely that the Lords were sympathetic to her case because they had grown tired of dealing with her obstinate husband. She had simply been trying to sue for a separation in the ecclesiastical courts but her husband was using his position as a peer to claim he was exempt from the ruling. While the Lords first attempted to mediate a reconciliation, the Countess was only able to appear once the Lords provided a guarantee that her husband would not seize and imprison her, yet once she appeared, she was successful in persuading the Lords to grant her both a separation and maintenance.

A divorce did not necessarily mean that a woman became destitute. This is perhaps one of the most important questions to ask in a time when a woman's financial security could be completely tied up with that of her husband's. Financial considerations were not always a problem for divorced women. Parliament could order maintenance to be paid to wives in the process of divorce actions. The Duchess of Norfolk petitioned the House of Lords for financial support, 'According to the custome and practice of the Ecclesiastical Court, in matrymoniall Causes... The plaintiff is Oblidgd to pay weekly to the Defendant such Sums of Money as shall be thought sufficient to Defend the same'.[113] This was not necessary, as she had maintained control over her own independent fortune as a baroness in her own right. Nevertheless, she claimed that she could no longer support herself as the charge was 'very great' and therefore it was necessary to 'pay her such sums of Money as your Lordships shall think sufficient for her Expenses'.[114]

Similarly, depending on circumstances, husbands did not retain all their wives' property after the divorce action was passed. Wealthy fathers would often have money placed into complex legal trusts which ensured that the money remained out of the husband's control, providing their daughter with an income independent of her husband. Depending on the circumstances, sometimes no financial loss occurred. Anne Macclesfield even had her marriage portion returned to her.[115] Not only did the Duke of Norfolk have to give back the Duchess's £10,000 dowry, but he had to cede control of the estates she had brought into the marriage. While money worries probably did act as a deterrent to wives seeking separation, it was not always insurmountable.

Perhaps one of the most surprising aspects of divorce cases was that men could also be criticised for what was seen as inappropriate behaviour. Women were not always blamed for the breakdown of a marriage, and men did not always escape public censure. It was not a simple matter of dominance and oppression. Instead, people had clear expectations of how both sexes should behave and this was often manipulated by both men and women in order to separate from their partners. Members of the House of Lords objected to granting the Duke of Norfolk a divorce on the grounds of adultery, on the basis that he too had been unfaithful to his wife.

The Duke offered up a conventional defence, saying that: 'A man by his folly brings no spurious issue to inherit the land of his wife, but a woman deprives her husband of any legitimate issue'. In other words, his adulterous affairs were acceptable because he could not disturb the inheritance of family property or domestic life through passing off his illegitimate children as belonging to his wife. This was not, however, particularly well received by the Lords. One member, Sir Thomas Powys, retorted that men: 'Bring home that to their wives which sticks longer by them than their children', which was a reference to sexually transmitted diseases. Thomas Powys clearly wanted to make the point that male adultery could also have a devastating effect upon the family. Sleeping around could be seen as being emasculating. Contemporary theorists taught that one of the defining characteristics of male superiority was control over himself. Lack of sexual self-control was therefore seen by contemporaries as being a feminine failing, losing him respect.

Another case in which male adultery scuppered a divorce case was that of the Calverts in 1710. Although Leonard Calvert had numerous witnesses to his wife's adultery, he abruptly dropped the case. He had no financial problems, no relatives who seem to have been able to influence him, and he was shortly to abandon his Catholic faith in order to take up the proprietorship of the province of Maryland. The only logical reason for him to do so when he was so desperate for both a divorce and to be revenged upon Charlotte is that his own adultery and cruelty had made Parliament extremely unlikely to grant him a divorce. He had not only had his own affairs, including a longstanding relationship with a neighbour, Mary Grove, but had been exceptionally abusive towards Charlotte. He was extremely verbally offensive to her, once saying: 'I had rather drink a glass of your blood than the best wine in the world'.

He would also attempt to terrorise her, by wandering around the house armed with weapons asking where she was hiding; once chasing her through the house brandishing a sword. One of the most memorable occasions occurred in 1702, when he turned a pregnant Charlotte out of the house at one o'clock in the morning, following her through the streets until she was taken under the protection of a night watchman. The numerous witnesses able to testify to all of these events would certainly have made obtaining a divorce, with himself portrayed as the innocent party, very difficult for Leonard Calvert. The sexual double standard was not as overwhelmingly powerful as has been previously believed.

To try and anticipate this, men would often start their divorce petitions with an account of their virtues as a husband and father. When Sir Patrick Blake petitioned for divorce in 1778, he was at pains to stress the former happiness of his marriage and that he continued to provide a fairly luxurious lifestyle. The Blakes had moved to the island of St Christopher in the West Indies in 1772. When Sir Patrick's business interests started to fail, he felt that his continued presence was needed there in order to avoid a complete financial collapse. Three years later, Lady Blake travelled back to England alone. While in England, Annabella Blake met an MP called George Boscawen in March 1776 and they started an affair. The Blakes' marriage had definitively broken down, as only two months later, on 12 May, Annabella ran away from one of Sir Patrick's houses at four o'clock in the morning. She met her lover at a pub in Essex, in a subterfuge where he used the fictitious name of Richard Thompson and she had concocted a somewhat bizarre cover story about a friend who had fallen ill, and who wished to see her again. Eventually they took up residence in France, where they lived openly together.

Sir Patrick defined their marriage as being one of companionship, describing how when he originally left England on business in December 1772, his wife 'accompanyed' him, only returning to England 'for the purpose of attending the education of her children'. Here, Sir Patrick paints a picture of an harmonious and supportive marriage, where the couple only separated when circumstances forced them to do so. He described himself as behaving with 'the most constant love and affection' and stated that this was mutual, with their 'constant' correspondence showing signs of the 'warmest affection'. He depicted himself as a generous provider, saying that until she eloped she continued to live in his properties with 'ample Credit',[116] by which he means that Lady Blake had enough money to keep up the status that the wife of a baronet would require.

By highlighting his continued provision of housing and money, Sir Patrick demonstrates his virtues as a husband and throws Lady Blake's own alleged failings into sharp relief. Afterwards, the petition goes on to cast Lady Blake as a bad mother, repeating that she only left Sir Patrick as her children 'required the care and Superintendence of their parents'[117] which would indicate that Sir Patrick and/or his lawyers were twisting contemporary expectations of women to their advantage. By the late eighteenth century, the idea had evolved that women were expected to have an immediate, deep connection to their children. Instead Lady Blake is portrayed as an unnatural woman, who abandoned her children for her own selfish reasons at a time when they greatly needed her care.

It is difficult to work out exactly how much a divorce would have affected a woman socially. It would certainly have affected a man very little, although a bad reputation might make some parents reluctant to encourage or sanction another potential match. This, however, might have been overcome by the promise of a title or a large income, depending on the scruples of the parents, girl and suitor in question. For women, however, the situation was more complicated. The most common assumption is that women were isolated from society. In *Mansfield Park*, Jane Austen banishes the former Mrs Rushworth to a 'remote and private' house which is cut off, not just from society but from her own family.

In real life, however, Jane Austen came across divorcees in a social setting. She writes to her sister Cassandra in 1801 about a ball at the Upper Rooms in Bath, where she sees the Honourable Mary-Cassandra Twistleton, who had been divorced two years previously on the grounds of her own adultery, saying: 'I have a very good eye for an Adulteress, for tho' repeatedly assured that another in the same party was the same she, I fixed upon the right one from the first'.

While Austen clearly did not encounter divorcees in everyday life, Mary-Cassandra Twistleton was certainly not cut off from society. Similarly, Lady Diana Spencer may have lost her position as Lady-in-

Waiting to Queen Charlotte but gathered around her a new literary and artistic circle of friends and managed to re-establish some of her old social contacts after 'a while'. She was also welcome at Devonshire House, where she was part of the same circle as her cousin, Georgiana, Duchess of Devonshire. By contrast, the Duchess of Grafton withdrew from London society after her divorce and re-marriage. Her friends 'had no thought of bringing her to court' and there was annoyed murmuring that the former Duchess, now the Countess of Ossory, had 'never looked better'. Even the King was heard muttering about whether divorced ladies should be permitted to marry again.

The one certainty in divorce cases is that women would lose custody of any children that their husband was willing to accept as his own. Even when women had been deemed innocent of any wrongdoing, the law saw itself as powerless to intervene if a father saw fit to retain his children and deny their mother access. Women who had been convicted of adultery were guaranteed to lose custody of their children. This was, famously, the reason that Georgiana, Duchess of Devonshire, gave up her lover Charles, Earl Grey. The Duke of Devonshire told her that she would never see their children – aged nine, seven and two – again if she did not both renounce Grey and give up her baby daughter fathered by Grey for adoption. She was forced to travel to France to give birth, remaining there until the Duke had forgiven her for her affair. Georgiana wrote rather piteously to her friend Lady Melbourne that, 'I have in leaving him for ever, left my heart and soul; but it is over now… he has one consolation, that I have given him up for my children only'.[118]

Similarly, Anne, Duchess of Grafton, whose affair with the Earl of Ossory was uncovered when the Duke sent teams of detectives to surround the house and collect evidence of her adultery, wrote, 'if it is not thought absolutely improper, I hope to be permitted some time to see my poor children, who are continually in my thoughts, and the loss of whom I can never forget; any other loss, God knows, is hardly felt in comparison'.[119] Despite this, it does not appear that she saw any of her children with the Duke again until she was on her deathbed 30 years later, when her son, Lord Euston, agreed to visit her. There does not seem to have been any further contact after her divorce with her two other children, Georgiana and Charles.

Child custody would, inadvertently, help lead to divorce reform through an indomitable, determined woman named Caroline Norton, whose life was recently explored in Diane Atkinson's biography *The Criminal Conversation of Mrs Norton*. As we have previously seen, in 1836 Mrs Norton was accused of adultery with the then Prime Minister, Lord Melbourne. Despite the collapse of the criminal conversation trial, George Norton still had the right to refuse Caroline access to their children. She seems to have been working under the assumption that they would share custody of the children, enjoying equal access and rights over them.

It is uncertain whether Caroline Norton actually believed that she had legal rights to the children, or whether she had decided that operating from a position of confidence gave her the best chance of success. She was later to write that 'it is a common error to suppose that every mother has a right to the custody of her children'.[120] In fact, the law as it then stood gave fathers automatic custody over children irrespective of whether they had been found guilty of cruelty, adultery – or anything worse! Mothers had no rights of redress. While some mothers had attempted to challenge this ruling, none had been successful in retaining their children.

The Nortons' letters during this period are a long series of negotiations regarding access to the children and financial arrangements. Both parties wished to agree upon the latter, giving Caroline a regular income and absolving George from being responsible for her debts. Access to the children soon became caught up with this matter. Caroline refused to discuss any potential financial agreement until she saw her children, while George insisted that their finances had to be clarified before any visits could be arranged. Losing hope that any arrangement could be reached amicably, Caroline embarked on a series of attempts to see them, watching the house and following them when they were taken for walks in the park. On another occasion she managed to force her way past the footman to see the children. These attempts could only give her fleeting contact, however, and simply made the children's caretakers more vigilant. The most horrifying situation occurred in 1837, when Caroline gained access to her children, who had contracted measles, at her brother-in-law's house when he was absent. After he came back, one of her children was forcibly pulled away from her while the other two ran away, screaming in terror, and Lord Grantley 'shook her fiercely', throwing her out of the house. After this incident, the children were then locked away where she could not gain access to them.

The futility of any attempts at negotiation led Caroline to embark on a campaign to have the laws regarding child custody changed. She aimed to give women who had been found innocent of adultery primary custody of their children under the age of seven and visitation rights to older children. Caroline had hundreds of years of legal and social precedents against her, but she was also a formidable opponent with a reputation as an implacable woman and a well-regarded writer. Caroline began to write pamphlets in favour of a proposed bill to modify these rules, and canvassed influential politicians to vote in favour of the Infant Custody Bill. One pamphlet was *The Law Relating to the Custody of Infants,* written in 1838. It was seen as being so incendiary that her usual publishers had refused to print it, fearing prosecution, and Caroline had to borrow money to have it printed privately. She initially gave logical arguments against fathers automatically retaining custody, pointing out that some men used their children solely as a 'means of persecution' and an 'instrument of vengeance' against their wives. She used vivid imagery and emotive language to depict one case where the father had removed a baby from its mother while it was in the act of being breastfed, describing it as an 'unnatural and revolting strife, the father tearing the child from its mother's breast, the mother, fleeing like a hunted hind'.[121]

If Caroline's skill as a writer was in her favour, so too was the fact that her case had been such a high profile one. A *Times* editorial drew attention to the fact that, although both Lord Melbourne and Mrs Norton had been 'equally acquitted', the lady was currently in an 'unfortunate condition', while the Prime Minister had experienced political good luck. The fact that the bill was so publicly intertwined with the fate of Mrs Norton gave the story greater resonance in people's minds, directly influencing the outcome. Although the bill failed the first time it was presented to Parliament, it passed the second time it was introduced, despite objections that women would be more likely to leave their marriages if they knew that they might retain their children. Even so, the bill failed to provide for women found guilty of adultery in a court of law, who continued to be deemed unfit to raise their children.   .

Caroline Norton's trial for criminal conversation with Lord Melbourne was a notable occasion when servant testimony was rejected. A body of damaging and incriminating evidence had been gathered by George Norton's formidable legal team, but the witnesses were deemed not to be credible. The team appears to have been directed by Norton's brother, Lord Grantley. As an ardent Tory, Grantley would have had an interest in ruining Lord Melbourne's reputation, thus bringing down his government and also ridding himself of a sister-in-law for whom he did not care.

Much of the evidence in the case seemed suspiciously similar to evidence given at other trials. The most damaging testimony came from servants who had been interviewed by George Norton's legal team. Lord Melbourne was often observed to enter the house through the back door, while callers would have been expected to enter through the public entrance. Thomas Tucker, a footman, claimed that when Lord Melbourne visited, no one else was allowed to intrude upon their meetings, not even 'intimate friends and relations'. Caroline took great care preparing her hair and makeup for Lord Melbourne's visits, and frequently became suspiciously dishevelled during the course of their time together. Ellen Monk, the Norton children's nurse, testified that Lord Melbourne had visited Mrs Norton in her bedroom, with the door bolted, when she was ill. Another servant, Ann Cummins, testified that Lord Melbourne had visited Mrs Norton after the birth of her second child and had said that the baby was 'not like [George] Norton'. This was intended to plant suspicion in the jury's eyes regarding the paternity of the baby.

Yet, the evidence of John Fluke, a groom, was the most damning.

He claimed that he had seen Lord Melbourne sitting in a chair while Mrs Norton lay on the floor with her dress raised to expose her thighs. Melbourne's legal team used the fact that Caroline had him sacked for drunkenness and that he was beset by financial problems, to discredit his testimony. He was also employed by another member of the Norton family, and had been overheard calling Caroline a damned bitch and that he would receive between £500 and £600 (worth approximately £50,000 today) if he successfully incriminated both Lord Melbourne and Mrs Norton. Ann Cummins also admitted that she had been put under pressure to provide suitable evidence and that she had been 'examined' by prosecuting lawyers several times before the trial. Additionally, all the witnesses were being given free accommodation by Lord Grantley. The fact that all the evidence came from servants who had been dismissed by the Nortons; the clear signs that witnesses had been tampered with; as well as the lack of any incriminating evidence for the previous two years, meant that their evidence was not deemed reliable and George Norton's plans for a parliamentary divorce collapsed.

Servants did not always band together, as seen in the divorce of Lady Diana Spencer. This Lady Diana, also disappointed in her marriage and her husband, would divorce her husband under intense public scrutiny. Lady Diana, commonly known as 'Lady Di', had married Viscount Bolingbroke in 1757. He had originally proposed as a throwaway joke while they were both attending the theatre with a large party, but had afterwards 'made a serious affair of it'.[122]

The marriage seems to have been a matter of convenience. He had been having a long-standing affair with a married woman, Lady Coventry, and his friends and family had started to worry that Lord Coventry could sue for divorce on the basis of his wife's adultery with Lord Bolingbroke, potentially leaving him liable to pay a large sum in financial compensation, and placing him under social pressure to marry Lady Coventry.

The marriage had broken down by 1772, amid rumours of drunkenness and violence, and the magazine *Town and Country* claimed that his 'irregularities', by which they meant adulterous affairs, 'excited her Ladyship to resolve upon retaliation'. The marriage finally broke down when Lady Di left the family home to put herself under her brother's protection, when he provided a home and financial support. Lord Bolingbroke's attempts to have her friends intercede and persuade her to return by 'preaching the doctrine of reconciliation'[123] completely failed. Lady Sarah Bunbury wrote:

Both sides are mad, I believe… As I heard he had got a woman in the house already, I can't say I do [pity him]. For if he was unhappy at the thought of having used her so cruelly as he had done, surely a man that had any feeling would not recover his spirits so easily.[124]

The divorce, however, came about because Lady Di had started an affair with Topham Beauclerk, a great-grandson of Charles II and his mistress Nell Gwynne. While most of the servants were willing to testify that they had been suspicious of the couple, one servant, Mary Lees, was ready to deny the existence of any abnormal behaviour. Some servants claimed that callers were denied access to the house when Topham was visiting, but Mary Lees denied that any such instructions were given. Similarly, debate took place about a couch which had been in the room during these visits, and whether the sides could be folded down so that it could be used as a bed. Again, Mary Lees contradicted the other servants when they said that this was possible. She also denied reports that the door had been locked or that dirty shoe marks had been found on the couch after the couple had exited the room, looking dishevelled.

The only indisputable proof that an adulterous affair had taken place occurred when Lady Di became pregnant. Although the loyal Mary Lees attempted to claim that Lady Di's stomach had swollen due to dropsy, it was obvious that she was heavily pregnant. She engaged the services of an obstetrician, Dr William Hunter, who had, somewhat paradoxically, become known for his reputation for discretion and had previously tried to help the Duchess of Grafton conceal her pregnancy by removing the child and arranging for it to be cared for by a wet-nurse. It is possible that they attempted to terminate the pregnancy. Mysterious boxes of medicine were delivered from London to Buckinghamshire, where they were then residing, instead of being obtained locally. Topham was the only person allowed to touch the box and he removed the labels from the bottles before they were given to Lady Di.

Any remedies, however, proved useless and arrangements had to be made to conceal the impending birth. Preparations were made to close the house, dismiss the servants and for her to give birth in the country but the child arrived before it was expected and the news quickly spread that Lady Di had had a child who had clearly not been fathered by her husband. Horace Walpole, who seems to have been well informed about the state of the Bolingbroke marriage, wrote that the divorce 'is determined; and by the consent of her family she is to marry Mr Beauclerk'. This suggests that there may have been a degree of collusion to dissolve the marriage. This does raise the question of why Mary Lees attempted to deny her mistress's guilt. However it is possible that Lady Di was trying to portray herself as a reluctant divorcee in order to avoid allegations of collusion. The divorce passed, leaving her free to marry her lover but this second marriage, despite the fact that it survived, appears to have been equally unhappy.

Servant testimonies turned trials for adultery into public entertainment for the masses, highlighting the instrumental role servants played in uncovering their employers' transgressions. In Jane Austen's *Mansfield Park*, Maria Bertram's affair is initially uncovered because her mother-in-law's maidservant, who has heard of her affair through a servants' gossip network, threatens to expose her. Austen's dramatic use of a servant threatening to reveal the affair closely follows many of the cases described in the newspapers at the time, suggesting that adultery being exposed by servants was a recognised phenomenon.

These 'real life dramas' were so popular that in 1780 a selection of adultery trials were printed under the title, *Trials For Adultery*. The title page promises many 'ridiculous, whimsical, and extraordinary' accounts, all 'fairly represented'. Another publication was the

Criminal Conversation Gazette, which endeavoured to collect the most notorious trials. Many of these focused on the servants, and how their testimony had brought the ladies' evil, amoral and reprehensible actions to light.

Lawrence Stone has described how the emphasis laid on moral instruction meant that divorce trial transcripts became a substitute for the novel. Stenographic records were also printed in individual pamphlets, and as newspaper and magazine articles. Some participants in trials even used newspapers as a way of presenting their own, often highly partisan version of the case. In 1793, William Middleton arranged to have a 'racy description' of his wife's alleged adultery printed in the *Bon Ton* magazine in order to sway public opinion in his favour. Adultery trial accounts were easily accessible to the literate British population. By 1820, at Queen Caroline's trial for adultery, one writer commented that 'you may look upon the British public as constantly occupied in reading trials for adultery'. In 1836, it took under 24 hours to publish a sixpenny souvenir of the *Extraordinary Trial!, with a portrait and memoir of the Honourable Mrs Norton.* Demand for access to the actual proceedings was also extraordinary. The *Morning Chronicle* reported that the galleries had been filled even before the doors had officially opened, and seats in the courtroom were being sold for up to ten guineas each, equivalent to approximately £640 today.

Trials for adultery were also depicted in popular prints, making them accessible to the illiterate and semi-literate sections of the population. Cartoons showed women being caught in the adulterous act and criminal conversation trials taking place. One cartoon from 1818 shows a woman dressed in a ridiculously short, very low cut dress, being interrogated in a court regarding her evidence of adultery. The eager and slightly ridiculous expressions on the judges' faces gives the impression that this process is taking place so that the judges can hear the salacious details. The caption asks whether the witness can be sure that the lady cried 'murder' or 'further'. It becomes clear that the cartoon is intended to make fun at the process of divorce, and how the trials delved into the details of people's lives. Another source is a print from 1797, which shows an adulterous wife trying to entice her lover to sleep with her, but the lover replies: 'Would if I could – can't afford it', referring to the high sums that lovers were ordered to pay to the husband in damages. Adultery and marital breakdowns were no longer a private matter.

The eighteenth century Duchess of Beaufort had an intriguing defence against her husband's divorce action. At the same time that the Duke sued for separation, she counter-sued for an annulment on the grounds that the Duke was impotent and that their marriage had never been consummated. It was an extremely clever defence. The usual test in such situations, a medical examination to try and ascertain whether the lady in question was a virgin or not, was clearly impossible. As it had already been proved that the Duchess had given birth to an illegitimate child, there was no way of categorically disproving her case.

The Duke attempted to fight back by producing letters in which the Duchess claimed how happy she was in her married life, which he alleged showed she was sexually satisfied, but this could not be proved to refer to sex. He produced witnesses to testify that the couple had always shared the same bed, but this too was not definitive proof that intercourse had taken place. The strongest piece of evidence came from servants who had dealt with the laundry and were prepared to testify that there were marks on the sheets and nightwear.

The judges themselves were unsure. The first court rejected the Duchess's case, but it was then upheld on appeal. The case was only resolved when, to everyone's shock, the Duke offered to undergo the canon-law test of virility, a test that had been used in the medieval era to indicate whether or not a husband was capable of having sexual intercourse. In this test, a man had to prove that he was capable of consummating a marriage by either going to a brothel or masturbating in front of witnesses. By 1743, this test was seen as archaic and had fallen into disuse. The Duke's willingness to undergo the test, and his successful performance, amazed many. Sir Horace Mann's reaction was typical. 'The Duke of Beaufort's victory, I think, was very great. I should certainly never have been potent behind the screen, on such an occasion'. Similarly, Horace Walpole referred to it as a 'victory... he, with more than mortal courage, stood the trial'. The Duchess's case collapsed, leaving the Duke free to obtain his divorce.

From the first trailblazing divorces in the 1690s, divorce had become a more regular occurrence. More women had the legal protection and the necessary power to end their marriages in the pursuit of their personal happiness. This did not, however, mean that life after divorce was guaranteed to be happy. After Topham Beauclerk died, leaving Lady Diana a free woman for the first time in 23 years, Edmund Burke observed her feeling of freedom:

> *I never, myself, so much enjoyed the sight of happiness in another, as in that woman when I first saw her after the death of her husband. It was really enlivening to behold her placed in that sweet house, released from all her cares, a thousand pounds a year at her own disposal, and − her husband was dead! Oh, it was pleasant, it was delightful to see her enjoyment of her situation.*[125]

CHAPTER 6

Wife Sales:
Disgraceful Transactions

' Gentlemen, it is her wish as well as mine to part for ever. She has been to me only a bosom serpent. I took her for my comfort and the good of my house but she has become my tormentor, a domestic curse, a night invasion, and a daily devil'.[126] This was reportedly the somewhat dubious sales pitch given by one husband, a Cumbrian farmer named Thompson, just before he sold his wife at market in Carlisle in 1832.

A wife sale was a process that took place in order to break an existing marriage by selling the woman to another man. Surviving evidence clearly demonstrates that wife sales began to take on an official, ritualised form during the late seventeenth century. Customs associated with the sale of cattle were used by couples engaging in wife sales, in order to create and legitimise their own form of unofficial, accessible divorce. Firstly, the wife had a halter placed around her neck, then she was led through various turnpikes, paying a charge at each one, before she was brought to the marketplace and sold to the highest bidder in an auction, sometimes by her weight.[127] There was a widespread belief that a halter was necessary to make the sale legal.

Once the sale had taken place, the woman was considered to be married to her purchaser. In the 1870s, a lawyer asked a woman bought at a wife sale and now seeking maintenance from her husband if he had put a rope around her neck, in order to determine the validity of the sale. Similarly, in the early nineteenth century a husband named Henry Frise burst out in court:

Her's my wife, as sure as we were spliced at the altar, for and because I paid half a crown, and I never took off the halter till her was in my house; lor' bless yer honours, you may ask any one if that ain't marriage, good, sound, and Christian, and everyone will tell you it is.[128]

The sudden increase in reports of wife sales around the time when parliamentary divorces were increasing in number indicates that ordinary people saw wife sales as their equivalent of a full divorce. For the majority who did not have the necessary money to obtain a parliamentary divorce but wished to separate from their spouse forever, a wife sale could provide them with the permanent closure that they sought. Wife sales started to decline around 1850, but cases were recorded as late as the twentieth century. In 1919, a lady from Tottenham told a group of magistrates that her husband had sold her, and an attempted wife sale reportedly took place in Northumberland as late as 1972.

The origins of the wife sale process are shrouded in mystery. Historians have identified potential cases as early as 1073, with the first substantiated case occurring in 1553. It may have originated out of ancient Anglo-Saxon traditions, which required the groom to pay his bride's family a sum of money before the wedding, known as a 'bridal-price'. Others have linked it to the rise of criminal conversation cases, where husbands were financially compensated for their wives' adultery, or the return of soldiers from the Napoleonic Wars, who found that their wives had moved on in their absence and wished to formalise the dissolution of the marriage. The existence of documented wife sales in the early sixteenth century, however, means that wife sales had already been in carried out for at least 200 years. It may be that external circumstances encouraged a resurgence of an earlier practice that had almost faded away. Intriguingly, historian Samuel Menefee, in his book *Wives For Sale,* recorded evidence that wife sales in France were regarded as a 'foreign' and 'peculiarly English'[129] practice.

It is impossible to determine exactly how widespread wife sales were. Historian Olwen Hufton concluded that there was 'very sparse evidence'[130] to suggest the existence of wife sales in *The Prospect Before Her*. Samuel Menefee, however, found evidence of nearly 100 different reported cases, all supported by various documents, from as early as the thirteenth century. It is also practically impossible to discover exactly how popular wife sales were, as it is unlikely that all cases were reported. Wife sales that were not considered newsworthy or those that did not come to the attention of the press and/or authorities would have left no trace.

Although there were few cases listed before the late eighteenth century, there is a very clear description of a ritual wife sale in Elizabeth Chudleigh's 1777 book *The Laws Respecting Women*. It is difficult to imagine the author simply inventing this, which would indicate that, while not all cases were documented, wife sales were in fact occurring in sufficient numbers to gain a decided notoriety. Contemporaries certainly believed that wife sales had increased rapidly during the eighteenth century. References were made in Derbyshire to sales in 'the usual way which has been lately practiced',[131] indicating that wife sales had spread into areas where they had been previously unknown. Similarly, in Birmingham officials said 'the sale of wives have of late frequently occurred among the lower class of people'.[132]

Changes in marital law at this time may have caused wife sales to increase in number. The 1753 Marriage Act tightened state controls on marriage in an attempt to eliminate clandestine and Fleet marriages, making it harder for people to simply deny their marriages had existed. Simultaneously, the collapse of the ecclesiastical courts formerly responsible for policing moral offences meant that there was decreasing Church control over marital separation. These factors made wife sales a more attractive option for those wishing to escape an unhappy marriage.

Wife sales were seen as a straightforward, public way of terminating a marriage and transferring responsibility for the lady to a new husband. Elizabeth Chudleigh wrote that wife sales were seen as a permanent dissolution of the marriage, 'the husband... as he imagines, at once absolves her and himself from all the obligations incident to marriage'.[133] The *Manchester Mercury* agreed, claiming that people had a 'vulgar notion'[134] that they no longer had any ties to their spouses after a wife sale.

Wife sales could, in theory, take place anywhere, but most seem to have occurred in areas such as fairs and markets. In some parts of the country, there was a widespread belief that a sale had to be public in order to dissolve the marriage successfully and form a new union, increasing the popularity of markets and fairs. One popular location was Smithfield Market in London, where at least 20 wife sales were held between the 1790s and the 1830s. In 1833, the *Bath Chronicle and Weekly Gazette* reported that a sale had been considered invalid, firstly because it had not taken place at market, and secondly because the purchaser had a wife already, necessitating a re-sale in Bath marketplace. Markets may have been used due to their links with livestock selling, but they could also offer a husband the opportunity to reach a larger potential customer base than normal. Some of whom would have travelled several miles and may have been more eager to take a potential wife on, not being aware of any gossip or local preconceptions regarding the lady's character or the breakdown of the marriage. Those who attended markets often had the financial means and the inclination to purchase something. Large numbers of people could also provide a convenient crowd for a husband to vanish into if he wanted to disappear.

At fairs, on the other hand, restraints were relaxed and sexual boundaries were transgressed, making it an ideal time to dispose of a wife in a slightly unorthodox way. The use of markets and fairs meant that an overwhelming majority of wife sales took place in urban areas. Sometimes, a particular site within a town would become known as a location for these sales, such as a market cross.

In the nineteenth century, inns and taverns seem to have taken over as the most popular location to hold a wife sale. Some inns even acquired a reputation for holding them, including the Castle Inn at Marlborough Castle in Wiltshire.[135] Alcohol, particularly beer and gin, is mentioned frequently in conjunction with wife sales, and featured prominently in the purchase agreements. The sums involved could be as little as a few glasses of beer, depending on the wealth of those involved, and the circumstances. In Towcester, in 1797, one wife was sold for £25, the equivalent of more than £800 today. At the other end of the spectrum, in Staffordshire, another wife was sold in 1823 for three gallons of ale.[136]

Wife sales did not necessarily follow the same conventions as a standard marriage. For example, some purchasers did not limit themselves to one wife, acquiring two at the same sale. Similarly, in Cornwall in 1835, two men clubbed together in order to purchase a woman they were presumably both keen on. Descriptions by both husbands and newspapers usually focused either on the women's physical beauty or their aptitude for hard work. Some husbands gave their wives a dowry to make them more appealing to potential buyers. One especially generous husband even continued to provide his former wife with an allowance after the death of her new partner. Not all the purchasers of a 'wife' were single. Occasionally, references are made to existing girlfriends or wives, suggesting that they were probably present at the moment of purchase. In 1837, one woman in Halifax physically attacked her husband after he bought a wife. Another 1768 purchase in Oxford ended in an argument between the buyer and his betrothed; however, relations were sufficiently mended soon afterwards for their own marriage to take place.

Husbands would often give a sales pitch in order to persuade other men that their wife was a desirable commodity. Sometimes the descriptions were humorous. A seller reported that amongst one Staffordshire woman's virtues was her ability to 'swear like a trooper, an' fight like a game cock'. Others were double-edged, such as this one by Cumbrian farmer Mr Thompson from April 1832:

She can read novels and milk cows... She can make butter and scold the maid, she can sing Moore's melodies and plait her frills and caps; she cannot make rum, gin, or whiskey, but she is a good judge of the quality, from long experience in tasting them.[137]

Sometimes, wife sales were advertised beforehand, with handwritten notices. One advert promised 'credit to any man who guarantees that his wife will not return to him'.[138] Newspaper advertisements were rare, presumably because they were expensive and could potentially invite unwelcome attention from officials trying to stop the sale, but one from 1796 read as follows:

> *To be sold for five shillings, my wife, Jane Hebland. She is stout built, stands firm on her posterns, and is sound wind and limb. She can sow and reap, hold a plough, and drive a team, and would answer any stout able men, that can hold a tight rein, for she is damned hard mouthed and headstrong; but, if properly managed would either lead or drive as tame as a rabbit. She now and then, if not watched, will make a false step. Her husband parts with her because she is too much for him.*[139]

One husband named Brooks advertised the imminent sale of his wife in Plymouth in 1822. A contemporary account of the sale explained that 'the report which accompanied the notice stated that the *lady* was not only young and handsome, but that she had rode to town in the morning on her own horse, of her own free will and accord, and with consent of her husband, who was to act the part of an auctioneer on the occasion; and that she would moreover, in the course of a few days, succeed to £600 which her husband could not touch'. This combination of money and good looks attracted an 'immense' crowd of potential buyers. Bids reached three pounds before the auction was broken up by two constables. On this occasion, however, the couple were expecting a specific man to purchase the lady. It may be that the advertisement was intended more to publicise the sale and consequent dissolution of the marriage, rather than attract potential purchasers. In this way, the sale screened the wife's passage from husband to lover.

On occasion, there could be cultural clashes between those at the bottom of the social spectrum, who saw wife sales as perfectly valid, and those higher up the social hierarchy, who were appalled by the process. This wife sale was broken up by the local law enforcement, which brought the husband up before the magistrate at the Guildhall. The husband seemed perplexed that the sale had been brought to an end, saying that 'he did not think there was any harm in it' and that 'many people in the country told him he could do it'. Similarly, his wife said that 'she had been told by different persons that the thing could be done by sale in the market place on a market day'.[140] The fact that their testimonies led to a 'good deal of consultation' may indicate that the authorities were undecided as to how severely they should be punished, if at all.

There were times when even sections of the elite were willing to sanction the process. Even some legal officials believed that wife sales were binding. An 'eminent Attorney'[141] was involved in drawing up a contract of sale, and another London attorney advised the husband, wife and prospective purchaser, that 'the sale would not be valid unless made in market overt'.[142] One contract later published in the *Worcester Chronicle* dating from July 1857 read, 'Thomas Middleton delivered up his wife Mary Middleton to Philip Rostins, and Sold her for one shilling and one quart of ale, and part wholy and solely for life, nor trouble one another for life'. [143]

On other occasions, the man overseeing the transaction would have official status, such as a market official or a poor law official. One magistrate said: 'As to the act of selling itself, I do not have a right to prevent it… it rests upon the custom preserved by the people, of which it would be dangerous to deprive them'.[144] One Yorkshireman's conviction in 1837 for his part in a wife sale 'caused widespread surprise and consternation'.[145] It seems likely that the unfortunate man was wholly unaware that wife sales were not recognised by all as being legitimate. Further evidence to suggest that these sales were commonly accepted comes with reports of the ringing of church bells to celebrate sales. Although it was not officially sanctioned, wife sales were accepted in varying degrees by local communities.

Poorer men were often unable to follow elite social codes, as these were based on the cultural norms of the elite, including marriage, economic independence from others and the governing of a household.

The vast majority of men did not own enough land to live independently and would seldom have been able to achieve complete economic independence from others, such as the local landowner. Many men were limited in their ability to marry and construct an independent household. Couples delayed their marriage until they had saved enough money to establish a household. Some men were even forbidden to marry. Those who were being trained in a trade, such as dressmaking for example, had to first serve out an apprenticeship, working for an established craftsman/craftswoman. Apprentices were forbidden to marry during their training, which usually lasted around seven years. This meant that poorer men and women were used to establishing and following their own conventions, where practices such as wife sales were considered perfectly acceptable.

As we have seen, many wife sales took place in alehouses, inns and taverns, which were popular meeting places for those further down the social scale. These places were seen as an area where social regulations could be ignored. The alehouse was an alternative form of society, where practices which were theoretically censured by the elite, such as adultery, became perfectly acceptable. Elite regulations against practices such as wife sales, seemed as irrelevant to ordinary people as they were unachievable, leading poorer men to form their own methods of marital separation.

Wife sales had entered the public imagination and some printers produced pamphlet accounts of wife sales to entertain the masses. Some included verses:

Come all you kind husbands who have scolding wives.
Who thro' living together are tired of your lives,
If you cannot persuade her nor good natur'd make her
Place a rope round her neck and to market pray take her.

Should any one bid, when she's offer'd for sale,
Let her go for a trifle lest she should get stale,
If six-pence be offer'd, and that's all can be had,
Let her go for the same rather than keep a lot bad.

Come all jolly neighbours, come dance sign and play,
Away to the wedding where we intend to drink tea;
All the world assembles, the young and the old,
For to see this fair beauty, as we have been told.

Here's success to the couple to keep up the fun,
May bumpers go round at the birth of a son;
Long life to them both, and in peace and content,
May their days and their nights for ever be spent. [146]

Different versions of this song were attached to printed accounts of wife sales and adapted to fit specific sales.

Women displayed a wide variety of reactions to being sold. Many played an active role in arranging their own sales. A wife sale in a public place could provide a façade of a public auction, in order to cover up a wife's affair and the fact that she no longer wished to cohabit with her husband. Many women seem to have been sold to their current lovers, rather than to unknown strangers. A description of life in 1815 England by the French writer Rene Pillet, informs us that 'the purchaser, always a widower or a youth, is usually a connoisseur of the merchandise for sale, who knows her; one only presents her at market as a matter of form'.

Even in Elizabeth Chudleigh's *The Laws Respecting Women*, written to argue against the degradation of women and to advocate greater women's rights, there is an acknowledgement that women played a large part in arranging these sales in conjunction with their husband, and sometimes the purchaser. Elizabeth Chudleigh writes that wife sales took place in cases where both the husband and wife were 'heartily tired of each other, and agree to part'. If even texts which detailed female subordination described a wife sale as an equal process, it seems likely that the process was, by and large, a mutually directed process. Elizabeth Chudleigh writes that:

a purchaser is generally provided beforehand on these
occasions; for it can hardly be supposed that the delicate female

would submit to such public indignity, unless she was sure of being purchased when brought to market.[147]

In most cases the wife seems to have been sold to a pre-arranged partner, often somebody with whom she had been cohabiting. There are numerous examples where the women had been previously acting as 'housekeepers' for their future purchasers, hinting at a relationship predating their sale.[148] One wife sale in Suffolk in 1789 had taken place shortly after the wife had given birth. On these occasions, the child was usually included in the sale, suggesting that there was at least some doubt about the child's paternity.

Somewhat bizarrely, some men agreed to take back their wives if the purchaser was not pleased with her. On 3 January 1815, John Osbourne sold his wife Mary, together with her child, for the sum of one pound at The Coal Barge tavern in Maidstone. He formalised this by having a deed drawn up with witnesses present and 'expressing his willingness to take his spouse again at any future period'.[149] As she was sold together with her child, it is likely that she was already having an affair with her future purchaser. It may be that this was a remark intended to wound her, suggesting that the new relationship would soon disintegrate, or perhaps he was desperately clinging on to the hope that they would reconcile. While reporting one 1832 wife sale, newspapers reported that the wife's purchaser had previously been romantically entangled with her.

Another indication that the wives had agreed to the purchase lies in the positive adjectives used to describe the women as they went through the process. The women being sold, are in 'high glee', 'very happy', 'much pleased' and 'eager'.[150] Rather than being dismayed or worried regarding the future, the women were happy with the impending demise of their marriages. Not all men, however, followed through on a promise to buy their lover. In the previously mentioned Plymouth sale, broken up by public officials, a man named Kane agreed to buy his presumed lover for £20, worth nearly £840 today. When he did not appear at the market, she arranged with the ostler of the local inn, with whom she seems to have been casually acquainted, to bid for her in his place.

On another occasion, a group of women intervened to protest when a wife sale was prevented. In Stockport in 1851, a wife 'at once consented' to be sold at a public sale to terminate her marriage. Her husband was violent, probably an alcoholic, and had been living with another woman for some time. When the sale was broken up by police intervention, 'many of the women, who really believed that the sale of a wife was strictly legal, complained of the interference of the police, and the hardships of a wife being prevented from relieving herself of a worthless husband'.[151] Many women seem to have believed that wife sales could empower a wife by freeing her from a failed marriage. Although the ritual itself was necessarily demeaning to women, this might not have been because men were actually treating their wives as property. While the use of halters and auctions makes the process seem degrading to modern eyes, some contemporary observers saw the process as an empowering one that allowed women to take control over their marriages and lives.

Some of the women, however, were given no choice. One report of an 1836 sale noted that the original husband had 'turned his wife and only child out of doors to shift for themselves', leaving his wife to seek out a man to support both her and the child. Drink seems to have played a large role in a number of cases. Another husband from Falmouth declared in 1833 that 'his only reason for parting with her was that he was more fond of [alcohol] than of the society of woman… [and] he wanted to have a good drop… that night'.[152]

Some, but not all of these husbands later repented and reportedly tried to purchase their wives back. One of these men was a repentant Warwickshire yeoman who sold his wife during the chaos of the Civil War. He later attempted to reconcile with her, only to find that she was enjoying life with her new husband so much that she refused to return home with him.[153] Another eighteenth century London husband named Higginson 'sold his wife in a fit of conjugal indifference' but was so devastated at his wife's refusal to leave her new purchaser after 'his most pressing solicitations' that he later committed suicide.[154]

Some lovers did not react positively to the news of a wife sale. Perhaps they thought the process degrading, or they suspected a plot to sell the wife to a third party. In November 1856, one husband, John Starkey, went to collect his wife from her lover's house in order to lead her to market for sale. Unfortunately for him, the man did not react well to the prospect of his lover being sold. He attacked Starkey, biting the abandoned husband on the cheek so fiercely that he began 'bleeding profusely'.[155] Starkey made his way to the marketplace to seek help but when the police made their appearance they recognised him as an army deserter and transported him to prison to await orders from the War Office.

One lady who underwent a traumatic wife sale experience was the wife of Bristol man Thomas Nash, who attempted to sell his wife to the highest bidder at a public auction in 1823, without any success. One published account of the sale states:

it was a long while before any one ventured to speak, at length a young man who thought it a pity to let her remain in the hands of her present owner generously bid six pence! In vain did the anxious seller look around for another bidding, no one could be found to advance one penny, and after extolling her qualities and warranting her sound, and free from vice, he was obliged... to let her go at that price.[156]

If this wasn't bad enough, 'the purchaser... soon repented of his bargain' once he realised he had taken on a new wife. He 'again offered her to sale' but she did not like the next new purchaser and made a hasty exit with her mother from what must have been a humiliating and frightening experience. In 1830, the *Morning Post* wrote that one Gloucestershire wife was 'inveigled' to market and surprised with the news that her husband had decided to sell her. He threw a halter around her neck but she managed to free herself and escape before a serious buyer could be found, while in Dartmouth one poor woman was dragged to the harbour for sale in 1817.

One especially ingenious Georgian wife outwardly accepted her husband's plan to sell her but decreed that she should be sold at Newcastle. At this time, the Napoleonic Wars were in their final stage but the government was still struggling to recruit enough men to fulfil the navy's requirements. They therefore created press gangs which were empowered to seize men from ports such as Newcastle and force them into naval service. She intentionally timed their journey so well 'that on his arrival, a press gang conveyed him on board a ship',[157] where the unfortunate husband was compelled to embark on a long voyage in the service of the British Navy.

More considerate husbands may have been trying to ensure their wife's future survival before leaving the area, either to go into the army or for other, more dubious purposes. On other occasions, purchaser, seller and wife had all come from the same town, despite having travelled many miles in order to reach the fair or market. Even if the purchaser had not previously been the wife's lover, in these cases it is likely that they were at least known to each other.

Examinations of wife sales tend to show that wives either maintained the same social standing or rose slightly in the social hierarchy. One of the most dramatic cases was that of the Duke of Chandos and Anne Wells, a chambermaid from Newbury. During the 1730s, the Duke was having dinner with a companion at the inn where Anne Wells worked. After they finished their meal, they noticed a disturbance outside and went to investigate. The explanation came that: 'A man is going to sell his wife and they are leading her up the yard with a halter round her neck'. 'We will go and see the sale', said the Duke. On entering the yard, however, he was 'so smitten with [Anne Wells's] beauty and the patient way she waited to be set free from her ill-conditioned husband, the inn's ostler, that he bought her himself'.

Initially, she became the Duke's mistress but within a decade both the Duke's wife and Anne's husband had died and they married at a chapel in Mayfair on Christmas Day, 1744. She was not universally accepted amongst the aristocracy; shortly after the marriage Lord Omery would say that: 'Of her person & character people speak variously, but all agree that both are very bad'.[158] Despite this, the wealth and luxury of her new life must have made up for any social shortcomings. A portrait of Anne, painted a year after her marriage, shows her dressed in satin, lace and pearls, wearing a peeress's robe, while her hand stretched towards her duchess's coronet, lying next to her on the table. Quite a step up for an inn chambermaid.

Their marriage seems to have been a happy one before Anne died 15 years later. When the Duchess died, the *Gentleman's Magazine* reported that as she lay dying, she 'had her whole household assembled, told them her history, and drew from it a touching moral of reliance on Providence; as from the most wretched situation, she had been suddenly raised to one of the greatest prosperity... and then dismissed them with gifts; dying almost in the very act'.

In general, people seem to have grown more and more hostile towards wife sales from the late eighteenth century onwards. Some couples were chased round the town, requiring the authorities to step in and protect them. In 1819, the *Manchester Mercury* wrote that in the previous years wife selling had started to be 'punished with laudable severity'. Accounts of the 1823 Bristol wife sale stated that the husband John Nash 'was obliged to make a precipitate retreat from the enraged populace'. As time progressed and severe Victorian morals slowly took over from eighteenth century licentiousness, the more prosperous seem to have shied away from using this tradition, leaving wife sales solely as the preserve of the lower classes. Growing abhorrence to the practice of wife selling can be seen through Thomas Hardy's 1886 novel *The Mayor of Casterbridge,* where a husband's drunken wife sale sets off a chain of events that will haunt his life forever.

Female mobs became increasingly common at wife sales. In Manchester, women reacted exceptionally badly to the announcement of an impending wife sale in 1824. The newspapers reported that 'the female part of the crowd, apprehensive of the dangerous effects of such a precedent and urged on by a proper feeling of the indignity offered them, determined upon a protest against so indecent a proceeding, and in the absence of pen, ink, and parchment, they recorded, with ample heaps of mud upon the faces of the cattle dealers, the burden of their indignant sentiments'.[159] This practice would later be reported in London and Somerset in the 1830s. It may be that as the number of wife sale cases grew, and awareness of the practice rose, women began to see it as more of a threat than previously.

Those men who were determined to sell their wives began to take ingenious steps to ensure that the wife sale would be allowed to proceed. In early 1846, a man named Sheer prepared to sell his wife at Callington, in Cornwall. Finding, however, that there was 'indignant feeling' against him in the marketplace, and that 'it was not unlikely that he would be treated to a ducking', he decided to organise a decoy. Shortly after, 'a friend of his, dressed in female attire, was led with a halter by a country-fellow into the marketplace'.[160] People simply assumed that this was the couple they had heard about, and such a large crowd gathered that the marketplace was thrown into chaos. Stalls were upset, goods were strewn across the marketplace, and 'a great number' were knocked to the ground and trodden on in the stampede. After this frenzied scene came to an end and the crowd dispersed, Sheer and his wife entered the marketplace, whereupon she was sold for two and a half shillings.

As attitudes became more conservative during the nineteenth century, and contemporary views changed, now perceiving women as weak, frail and in need of protection, people higher up the social scale also grew disgusted. One man wrote a letter to *The Times* in response to its report of an 1832 Cumbrian wife sale asking, 'Has the Magistrate no power to prevent such disgraceful exhibitions? The act of selling a wife by auction is unlawful, but the question is, ought it not to be prevented or punished as an offence against public decency and morals?'[161]

Wife sales began to be viewed as barbaric and outdated. In 1849, the *Preston Chronicle* wrote that a wife sale had taken place 'as was want in the old time',[162] indicating that the Victorians saw it as a relic of an uncivilised age. Similarly, the *Leicester Journal* was outraged that wife sales could take place 'in such civilised times'.[163] In 1819, the *Carlisle Patriot* reported that a man, John Lockett, had been sentenced to six months' imprisonment for attempting to sell his wife,

Ellen. They had only lived together for six weeks and the sale was by mutual agreement. The judges let him go free, as he had so obviously thought that the sale was legal, but when they were ordered to try and reconcile, Ellen Lockett adamantly refused, saying: 'Nay, I shanno'.[164]

Others later began to find selling a wife impossible. In 1845, when one man attempted to sell his wife to her lover, they were stopped twice, firstly by the presence of the police and secondly by an outraged lawyer, who not only refused to draw up a deed of sale but 'desired him to go to a place supposed to be much further off than the market-place'.[165]

Furthermore, there could be severe consequences for people engaged in wife sales if they came to the attention of the authorities, as one couple found out in February 1819. Seventeen years before, John Forman had sold his wife, Prudence, to Joseph Holmes. During that time, Prudence and Joseph had moved to another parish, lived happily together and had had three children, who were recognised and baptised as the offspring of a legitimately married couple. As far as we know, John Forman had no contact with his former wife until the authorities became aware of this situation. It appears likely that at some point, the Holmes family needed to seek financial assistance from their parish. This was an unpopular move, as local taxes increased when there were more people dependent on parish relief. When they did so, the Holmes' parish argued that their children were not the responsibility of the parish where they had been born and brought up. Instead, they argued that they were the responsibility of John Forman, Prudence's legal husband.

This sparked off a legal battle to determine exactly who was responsible for the children. Unfortunately for all concerned, the judge decided that children 'must be taken to be those of their legal parents' and, somewhat bizarrely considering the number of children bastardised by parliamentary divorces, that 'it would be monstrous' to declare the children illegitimate. Responsibility was taken away from their father and given to an unwilling stranger, and the children were forced to move away from the only home they had ever known. An unhappy ending for all concerned.[166]

151

To modern eyes, the thought of selling a spouse seems fantastical. The in-depth descriptions of the rituals of a wife sale, together with detailed reports of individual cases, demonstrate that wife sales were an option for separating couples. Enough of these reports have been linked back to documented individuals, such as the Duke of Chandos and Prudence Forman, to illustrate that they were not just a literary invention. Perhaps the most peculiar aspect of wife sales is the argument that they could be seen as empowering. As a form of separation open to ordinary people, they provided those who did not have the financial means to undergo a legal separation or a parliamentary divorce, a way of completely and permanently (as they believed) separating from his spouse.

Similarly, the group of women protesting at the termination of a wife sale shows that some women, at least, saw wife sales as the only possible way for the average woman to free herself from an unwanted marriage. A great many of the reports either openly state that the lady had been sold to a lover, or contain indications that an affair had taken place, either through the presence of a newborn child, or a prior link between the purchaser and the wife.

Wife sales are perhaps the strongest possible example of the massive gulf between the values of the pre-Victorian era and now. Today, it is almost impossible to believe that a woman being led round a marketplace in an animal halter, and sold by her weight at auction, could be seen as empowering.

Conclusion

In 1857, the Matrimonial Causes Act ended the jurisdiction of Parliament and Church Courts over divorces, transferring power instead to a civil court, making divorces simpler, easier and cheaper to obtain. Caroline Norton played an instrumental role in fighting for changes to divorce and custody law, campaigning for the new divorce act, and to protect the earnings and property of separated women from being seized by their husbands. Women now had the ability to sue their husbands for divorce if they could prove that they had been both unfaithful and cruel, or deserted their wife. The act also allowed separated women to function as if they were single, making contracts in their own right, inheriting and bequeathing property, and maintaining control of their own finances. Women could now also petition for custody of their children over the age of seven on a more equal basis with men. In 1858, the first full divorce was granted in the new Court of Matrimonial Causes.

It had become easier for middle class couples to divorce fully but poorer people found it had become more difficult to seek a formal separation. The costs of the new Court of Matrimonial Causes were beyond their means. The Court of Requests gave legal aid to poor applicants but it saw its last legal suit between husband and wife in the early seventeenth century. Afterwards, the rules against spouses suing each other were strictly enforced. This, juxtaposed with the demise of the local ecclesiastical courts, meant that legal separations were harder to come by for those with limited financial means. Wife sales, already beginning to fall out of favour, declined even more under Victorian censure. The death penalty for bigamy was officially abolished in 1861. In practice it had been forgotten long ago but nevertheless, punishment for bigamists remained harsh. Those found guilty were usually sentenced to transportation to Australia, or, after 1861, to seven years' penal servitude.

Changing attitudes did not only harm the 'average' person in society. Henry VIII executed his wives with relative ease but in the

1820s George IV found himself unable to divorce his wife, the licentious Queen Caroline, owing to public outrage.

What stands out in many of these cases is the immense courage and strength of the individuals involved. Some couples had simply grown apart and were separating by mutual agreement, but many others were women fleeing abuse. Their fates vary. Mary Bowes, Countess of Strathmore, succeeded in escaping from severe physical and emotional abuse with her fortune intact. Elizabeth Blood showed similar personal courage in fleeing her husband, Holcroft, but she found that his money and contacts were too difficult for her to beat. Other women, such as Clara Louisa Middleton, were not innocent parties. Clara Louisa carried on an affair with her servant John Rose, destroying innocent servants' careers and lives in the process. Similarly, Elizabeth Stafford had an affair with her husband's steward, and plotted to defraud her husband into the bargain. Some women had happy endings. Mary Duchess of Norfolk had a joyful, if short, marriage to her second husband, Sir John Germain. Similarly, Anne, Duchess of Grafton, remarried her lover, the Earl of Ossory, and appears to have lived happily with him until her death. In contrast, Lady Diana Spencer married her lover, Topham Beauclerk, but her subsequent marriage to him was not as fulfilling as she might have expected.

We remain ignorant of others' fates. Women such as Elizabeth Eggington, held prisoner by her husband, or Elizabeth Walter, whose husband stole her fortune, disappear from court records. We can only guess at what happened to them. Even more mysterious are the women who engaged in wife sales. The lack of documentation means that we know little about their lives. The anonymous woman who lured her husband into the path of a press gang when he threatened to sell her at market must have been a cunning character, but we do not even know her name. In many cases, we are allowed simply a glimpse into the life of the ordinary separated woman: being sold at a wife sale, angrily refusing to reconcile with a husband, plotting with the local community to save her goods from her husband. It is enough, however, to reveal the gumption, bravery and ingenuity of those who refused to simply live by society's rules and accept their marriages, and who strove to find a better life.

The Divorces of Henry VIII:
The Sharp'st Kind of Justice

Henry VIII's story of marital grief and discord fascinated people at the time and still does so today. After the execution of Katherine Howard, when people were debating whether he would search for a new wife or take back his discarded ex-wife, Anne of Cleves, a prominent court lady, Elizabeth Basset, burst out: 'What a man the king is! How many wives will he have?'

But despite the rhyme 'Divorced, beheaded, died. Divorced, beheaded, survived', Henry did not obtain a divorce as we would understand it, a declaration that the marriage had been legally dissolved. What Henry did obtain from three of his wives, Katherine of Aragon, Anne Boleyn and Anne of Cleves, was an annulment, a legal ruling declaring that the marriage had never existed. Though their marriages to Henry had all been terminated in the same way, each of these women met different ends. One died under house arrest, one was beheaded on Tower Green and the last died a great landowner, one of the richest ladies in England.

Historians have disputed whether Henry's interest in Anne Boleyn fuelled his desire for a divorce, or whether he had begun to think of ending his marriage to Queen Katherine before she arrived on the scene. Anne joined Queen Katherine's household as a Lady-in-Waiting in 1523 but their initial courtship was so secret that we cannot be sure exactly when it began. What we do know is that Henry's first instinct was not to make Anne his Queen. In the late 1520s, when Henry first began to write to Anne, his letters were those of a man courting a woman to be his mistress. Anne, however, had other ideas, and the only way that she would agree to commit to Henry was as his wife, not as his mistress. Katherine had to go.

Katherine of Aragon had previously married Henry's brother, Prince Arthur, at the age of 15 in 1501, but Arthur's sudden death in 1502 had left her free to marry Henry in 1509. Henry argued that this marriage had infringed Church Law. Many marriages which would be considered perfectly acceptable today were prohibited in the sixteenth century if people were even distantly related through either marriage or blood. The Old Testament book of Leviticus supported Henry's case, stating, 'If a man shall take his brother's wife, it is an unclean thing... they shall be childless'. This, Henry contended, was a clear reference to the fact that all the sons of the marriage had died either at birth or shortly after. He ignored the only survivor of Katherine's numerous pregnancies, Princess Mary, arguing that she did not count because she was a girl.

Unfortunately for Henry, another biblical book, Deuteronomy, stated the opposite. To complicate matters further, at the time of Prince Arthur's death it had been argued that Leviticus did not apply because Arthur and Katherine had not consummated their marriage before his early and unexpected death, possibly due to the sweating sickness, a mysterious disease that ravaged Europe during the sixteenth century. Katherine still maintained that this was the case and much of the investigations centred on the question of consummation.

It is difficult to ascertain whether Katherine was telling the truth about her virginity. Historians, influenced by Katherine's undeniably strong religious beliefs, have tended to support Katherine, seeing her as incapable of lying. There is, however, evidence that Katherine had previously lied about an early pregnancy, deliberately fudging the dates of a miscarriage in a letter to her father, King Ferdinand of Aragon. This indicates that she may not have been above stretching the truth if she felt it necessary. More concretely, before the death of Prince Arthur, there seems to have been little doubt in court circles that the marriage had been fully consummated. The morning after the wedding, Prince Arthur was overheard boasting to his chamberlain that he needed a cup of ale, saying: 'I have this Night been in the midst of Spain, which is a hot region'.[167] After Prince Arthur's death, Katherine was closely watched for a time for signs of pregnancy.

If there had been any doubt at the time, the couple would surely have been encouraged to fulfil their obligations. Without consummation, the marriage was not fully valid, and it could be annulled by either party at any time. This would have destroyed the Anglo-Spanish alliance, not to mention Katherine's future marriage prospects. Both Spanish and English court officials would therefore have been eager to ensure that the wedding night had proceeded according to plan. Katherine was deeply religious, leading her supporters to argue that it was impossible that she could have lied. Others, however, have pointed out that since her infancy, Katherine had been raised to think of herself as the Princess of Wales and future Queen of England. Under such circumstances, it is not inconceivable that she could have seen her lie as justified, in order to fulfil her ultimate destiny.

The case for the annulment was first heard at a secret ecclesiastical court in 1527, before Cardinal Wolsey and other high-ranking churchmen. After two weeks, the court announced that it was not competent to judge such a case, after which Henry appealed to the Pope to judge the validity of his marriage. Around this time, Katherine was warned by the Spanish ambassador that the King was making moves to have their marriage declared invalid. The legal battles would drag on for six long years, with Henry trying to overcome the numerous obstacles the Pope created to discourage Henry from pursuing the annulment. Eventually, in 1528, the Pope sent a representative, Cardinal Campeggio, in order to try the case, but it took eight months after Campeggio's arrival for the new court to open at Blackfriars in London. Katherine's heartfelt plea to the King and court won her many admirers, resonating across the centuries to the extent that it was immortalised in Shakespeare's play *Henry VIII*:

Sir, I desire you do me right and justice;
And to bestow your pity on me: for
I am a most poor woman, and a stranger,

157

Born out of your dominions; having here
No judge indifferent, nor no more assurance
Of equal friendship and proceeding. Alas, sir,
In what have I offended you? what cause
Hath my behaviour given to your displeasure,
That thus you should proceed to put me off,
And take your good grace from me? Heaven witness,
I have been to you a true and humble wife,
At all times to your will conformable;
Ever in fear to kindle your dislike,
Yea, subject to your countenance, glad or sorry
As I saw it inclined: when was the hour
I ever contradicted your desire,
Or made it not mine too? Or which of your friends
Have I not strove to love, although I knew
He were mine enemy? what friend of mine
That had to him derived your anger, did I
Continue in my liking? nay, gave notice
He was from thence discharged. Sir, call to mind
That I have been your wife, in this obedience,
Upward of twenty years, and have been blest
With many children by you: if, in the course
And process of this time, you can report,
And prove it too, against mine honour aught,
My bond to wedlock, or my love and duty,
Against your sacred person, in God's name,
Turn me away; and let the foul'st contempt
Shut door upon me, and so give me up
To the sharp'st kind of justice.[168]

On 23 July, just over a month after the court had been called, rumours spread that the court was ready to announce its verdict. As a result, the courtroom was packed with eager onlookers, including the King. Instead of announcing that the King's marriage to Katherine of Aragon was void, as Henry confidently expected, Campeggio

158

announced that the case was too complex for him to pronounce a verdict and referred the case back to Rome. Henry's 'great matter', as it was called by contemporaries, was to be decided by European politics. The Pope was under the power of Katherine's nephew, Emperor Charles V, and was not in a position to incur his wrath by having his aunt's marriage declared invalid.

Henry stormed out of the court in anger, but he was fortunate that his marital problems had coincided with the arrival of new religious reforms, which would develop into Protestantism. Henry did not particularly care for the new religious theories but he did like their belief that the monarch should be head of the Church, instead of devolving power to the Pope in Rome. In 1531, Henry called a Parliament that declared Henry, not the Pope, as Supreme Head of the Church. The hostile Archbishop Warham conveniently died in 1532, leaving Henry free to appoint an archbishop who supported the new religious ideas. In 1533, the new Archbishop of Canterbury, Archbishop Cranmer, unsurprisingly declared the marriage invalid, and that Henry was free to marry again.

Most of Europe was on Katherine's side, but this could not help her in England. She refused to accept her new, demoted status. She refused to take an oath of allegiance, recognising the authority of the Church of England and the right of Henry's children by Anne to succeed to the throne. Letters addressed to Katherine still exist today where she has angrily ripped the portion of the letter addressing her as Princess Dowager. As punishment for her stubbornness, Henry ordered Katherine's removal to Kimbolton Castle in Northamptonshire, where she was virtually imprisoned and periodically subjected to attempts to force her into taking the oath of allegiance. Katherine was petrified that she would be poisoned, and would only eat food cooked in her room in front of her by one of her own women. She lived in seclusion and was forbidden from seeing her daughter, Princess Mary, who was herself under great pressure to take the oath recognising her parents' marriage as unlawful and she herself a bastard.

Chapuys, the ambassador of Emperor Charles V, felt sure that Henry would ask Parliament to order the executions of both Katherine and Mary. Katherine was growing increasingly unwell under the strain. Her contemporaries suspected that she had been poisoned but it now seems likely that Katherine was suffering from cancer. It had been intended that she should take an oath on her deathbed, swearing that she had not consummated her marriage with Prince Arthur, but this never took place. It is impossible to know whether the oath was simply forgotten in the upheaval at Katherine's deathbed or whether Katherine decided that her soul would fare better avoiding the question of her marriage to Prince Arthur. She died in January 1536, four months before the execution of her nemesis, Anne Boleyn, tormented by thoughts that if she had acquiesced to Henry's demands for an annulment, the English Reformation might never have happened.

Ironically, the first sign that Anne's power might be beginning to weaken came with the death of Katherine of Aragon. Anne Boleyn, the most notorious of Henry VIII's wives, was the wife whose marriage came to the most shocking end. Anne is the only Queen in British history to be condemned to death on the grounds of incest. At the time, however, Anne saw Katherine's death as a blessing, thinking that this, together with her new pregnancy, would smooth the way to her being accepted internationally as Queen of England. Both Anne and Henry dressed in yellow and threw a feast to celebrate Katherine's death with dancing. What Anne did not take into account, however, was that Katherine's death had, in a sense, set Henry free. If Henry had discarded Anne while Katherine was still alive, he would have come under great pressure to take Katherine back as his wife. Now, however, Henry could cast off Anne without suffering any repercussions. Many people had refused to recognise Anne as Henry's lawful wife, and there would be few impediments to having their marriage declared invalid.

Another barrier to their separation vanished when Anne miscarried a boy, on the same day that Katherine of Aragon was buried. Anne's obstetrical history after giving birth to Princess Elizabeth is somewhat unclear, but this was at least her second miscarriage. Her failure to produce an heir weakened Anne's position in two critical ways. Firstly, a lack of sons had been his justification for annulling his marriage to

Katherine of Aragon. This same failure in his marriage to Anne could easily lead him to the same conclusion. Secondly, if he had wanted to remove Anne before, there was now nothing stopping him from doing so.

Modern historians are still debating what exactly led to the downfall of Anne Boleyn, and how instrumental Henry was in arranging this breakdown. There is arguably little evidence to show that Anne had conclusively fallen out of favour. Just two weeks before Anne was arrested, Henry was pressuring Imperial ambassador Eustace Chapuys to recognise her as Queen. But by late April, Anne had guessed that there was something very wrong. The King spent hours secluded with his council, and crowds began to gather outside Greenwich Palace where they were staying, in anticipation of an important announcement. In later years, a witness would write to Anne's daughter, Elizabeth I, 'Alas, I shall never forget the sorrow I felt when I saw the sainted Queen, your most religious mother carrying you... in her arms... entreating the most serene King your father... The faces and gestures of the speakers plainly showed the King was angry'.[169]

That evening, it was announced that the King would not be going to Calais as planned and rumours started to circulate that something was amiss. Although most people did not know it then, Mark Smeaton, a musician in the Queen's household, had been arrested and was being questioned on suspicion of adultery. Smeaton confessed his guilt, but only after he had been 'grievously racked' for nearly four hours at the Tower of London. The next day, the King himself interrogated one of his friends, courtier Henry Norris, promising him a full pardon if he would confess to having an affair with the Queen. Among the others accused were William Brereton and Anne's brother, Viscount Rochford. The next day, 2 May 1536, Anne was taken from Greenwich Palace to the Tower of London, to await trial for adultery. Upon arriving at the tower, Anne broke down, alternating 'a great laughing' with hysterical bouts of weeping and praying.

This hysteria would provide Henry with even more evidence against Anne. She was guarded by five 'unsympathetic' women who were ordered to report to the Lieutenant of the Tower all Anne did and said. In her hysteria she talked wildly, searching through her memory of the past weeks to seek out anything that might incriminate her. She revealed that she had recently accused Henry Norris of being in love with her after a quarrel, saying: 'If aught came to the King but good, you would look to have me'.[170] Similarly, she revealed that a courtier named Francis Weston had been spending time in her apartments. Anne had thought Weston was having an affair with her cousin, Madge Shelton, but Weston had put an end to Anne's scolding, by claiming that: 'He loved one in her house better'[171] than Madge – Anne herself. It had been nothing more than a witty reply, designed to diffuse Anne's rebuke, but it provided further evidence against her and he, too, would soon be dispatched to the Tower.

The resounding lack of evidence has led most historians to absolve Anne from all the charges. A detailed list of times and places where adultery was committed was submitted to the court but the vast majority can be disproved, as Anne had been elsewhere at the time. The problem was that Anne had already overthrown so much of the old fabric of people's lives – Catholicism, Henry's marriage to Katherine, the old political order – that people were ready to believe her guilty of anything, even incest. Similarly, the imprisonment and subsequent release of other men, such as Sir Richard Page and Sir Thomas Wyatt, helped create the illusion that this was a genuine trial.

The indictment against Anne at her trial cast her as the sexual aggressor: 'She, following daily her frail and carnal lust, did falsely and traitorously procure by base conversations and kisses, touchings, gifts, and other infamous incitations, divers of the King's daily and familiar servants to be her adulterers and concubines' to the extent of committing incest with her brother, 'alluring him with her tongue in [his] mouth, and his tongue in hers'.[172]

Anne's trial for adultery and incest on 12 May 1536, was held three days after the rest of the accused had been found guilty. Anne's guilt was obviously pre-determined. She was found guilty of treason and sentenced to death, on the grounds that she had had liaisons with other men while married to the King. Anne's death would not be enough for Henry, however, who was determined to dissolve all ties to Anne.

Three days before her execution, Anne was visited by Archbishop Cranmer, who pronounced on the next day that her marriage to Henry had never been valid. In an unlikely coincidence, later on that same day it was announced that Anne would be granted a quicker death by being beheaded by an expert swordsman from Calais, as opposed to the axe or worse, burning alive.

It seems likely that Anne gave Cranmer some, possibly spurious, reason to declare her marriage invalid in return for a quicker death. Perhaps they declared it so due to the King's previous liaison with Anne's sister Mary, which made the marriage incestuous by sixteenth century standards, or maybe Anne acknowledged a pre-contract (betrothal) to another man. In July, Parliament would proclaim the marriage void because of 'certain just, true, and unlawful impediments'. Paradoxically, when Anne was executed for adultery on 19 May, describing her husband, on the scaffold, as 'a good, gentle, gracious and amiable King', officially she had never been the King's wife.

The annulment of Henry's marriage to his fourth wife, Anne of Cleves, occurred for simpler reasons. The story of Henry storming out of the room, shouting: 'I like her not!' and ordering Cromwell to find a way out of the betrothal, is one of the most memorable events in Tudor history. It is uncertain what it was about Anne that repelled the King so greatly; other ambassadors do not seem to have shared Henry's disgust towards her. Henry claimed that her portrait had unduly flattered her but another portrait painted of her, long after the annulment had been granted, does not differ greatly from the first painting.

Instead, it seems more likely that Anne had inadvertently insulted Henry. When Henry first met Anne, he went in disguise. Henry was trying to re-enact a scenario from chivalric romances where the lover visits his lady wearing a disguise. The lady was supposed to see through the disguise and recognise her lover. Anne, however, brought up in Cleves, was not familiar with the concept, nor had she ever seen Henry before. Some reports say that when Henry tried to kiss Anne, she reacted with disgust and pushed him away. Henry, famously narcissistic, was outraged at being summarily dismissed, and it seems likely that this inspired his great dislike of her.

The next day, after ranting to his attendants about Anne's inadequacies, saying: 'I see no such thing as hath been shown me of her, by pictures and report', he met Cromwell and asked him to find a 'remedy'. The wedding was postponed as Cromwell and Henry's council frantically searched for a pretext to call the wedding off without causing an international incident. They could not find a suitable excuse, however, and Anne and Henry were married on 6 January 1541. They did not consummate the marriage. The morning after the wedding, Henry complained that: 'Now I like her much worse. For I have felt her belly and her breasts... which struck me so to the heart when I felt them that I had neither will nor courage to proceed any further in other matters'.[173] The story inevitably spread around the court that Henry was unable to have sex with Anne – not, he stressed, because he was impotent. On the contrary, he felt himself: 'Able to do the act with others, but not with her'.[174]

Anne became a laughing stock, mocked by her ladies, who even felt able to interrogate her as to what was actually happening in the royal marital bed. One of the ladies, the Countess of Rutland, was especially blunt, saying: 'Madam, there must be more than this, or it will be long ere we have a Duke of York'.[175] Anne has often been portrayed as too naïve and ignorant to realise that there was anything wrong. Even before the marriage took place, however, Anne repeatedly tried to talk to Cromwell, an indication that she knew that things were not as they should be. Rebuffed, Anne turned to the Cleves ambassador, Karl Harst, complaining that the King was paying too much attention to one of her ladies-in-waiting, Katherine Howard. There was nothing that Harst could do, however, and by the time that Anne was ordered to leave court and move to Richmond Palace, the marriage was effectively over.

On 6 July, Anne was informed by a delegation that the King intended to have the validity of their marriage tried in an ecclesiastical court. The excuse used was that Anne had been previously betrothed to the son of the Duke of Lorraine. It was normal for Princes and

Princesses to be betrothed to several partners, particularly in childhood, before they eventually married. Betrothals were seen as a way of cementing foreign alliances. In a case such as Anne's, where the couple had not even met, let alone consummated the relationship, the betrothal would not normally have been sufficient grounds to break a subsequent marriage. Henry, however, had become used to having his own way, and no institution had the power to reject Henry's demands.

Anne seems to have tried to fight the annulment initially. When Henry demanded that Anne should send a written statement of her consent to the ecclesiastical investigation she refused, with 'tears and bitter cries'. Nevertheless, just 24 hours later, her resistance was at an end. Anne had the benefit of knowing how Henry's earlier discarded Queens had been treated and this may have induced her to accept Henry's offer. Anne also mentioned that she feared that someone 'would slay me' if she returned to Cleves. Presumably, she felt that her failure to please Henry would have angered powerful people in Cleves.

Anne, therefore, chose to accept Henry's offer of wealth, status and position, in return for relinquishing her marriage without a fight. She was offered a large income of £4,000 (the equivalent of £1.23 million), as well as the manors of Bletchingley and Richmond and, perhaps most significantly, Anne Boleyn's childhood home of Hever Castle. She wrote to Henry that 'though this case must needs be both hard and sorrowful for me, for the great love which I bear to your royal person', she was willing to accept the annulment of their marriage. Knowing that Henry was frightened of the possible political implications, she offered to let the King read any letters sent to her from abroad, and to answer them as the King directed. Cleverly, knowing Henry's flair for the dramatic, she reassured him of her acquiescence by sending him her wedding ring, 'desiring that it might be broken in pieces as a thing which she knew of no force nor value'.[176]

Anne was awarded the title of 'The King's Sister'. She got on well with her replacement, Katherine Howard. In 1541, she came to Court and the foreign ambassadors reported with amazement that not only did Anne show her former Lady-in-Waiting reverence by 'addressing the Queen on her knees',[177] but the two women danced merrily together, while the King, aged and infirm, looked on.

The fall of Henry VIII's fifth wife, Katherine Howard, was decidedly less complicated. She seems not to have excited as much political hostility as Henry's previous wives, possibly because the King was so enamoured with her that any action against her would have been suicidal. Ordering that a commemorative medal be struck in honour of Katherine, he called her his 'rose without a thorn'. By now Henry was 49, and Katherine, aged around 16, seems to have been his version of a midlife crisis. She was especially good at anticipating and fulfilling Henry's every wish, taking as her motto 'No other will than his'. This, together with her youth, was probably what captivated Henry. The French ambassador wrote that Henry 'is so enamoured of her that he cannot treat her well enough and caresses her more than he did the others'.

Katherine was, however, not wholly suited to being Queen of England. After the early death of her mother, Katherine had been taken into the household of her step-grandmother, the Dowager Duchess of Norfolk. Aristocratic children were often sent to another house for a time where they could be educated in music, reading and writing, and courtly behaviour, but the Dowager Duchess seems to have been content to allow her charges to run riot, with the result that Katherine was rather more sexually experienced than Henry would have expected. Her first affair was with her music teacher, Henry Manox. Katherine would later confess that: 'I suffered him at sundry times to handle and touch the secret parts of my body which neither became me with honesty to permit nor him to require'. Katherine later exchanged Manox for another man named Francis Dereham, whom Katherine said had: 'Lay with me naked and used me in such sort as a man doth his wife many and sundry times'.[178] Alison Weir has described her as an 'empty headed wanton' but this fails to take into account the fact that Katherine was extremely young, around 13, at the time of her first experience. Nevertheless, Katherine would have done well to cut all ties to her former life when she married Henry.

Instead, she gave positions in her household, not only to a former love rival, Joan Bulmer, but to Francis Dereham himself.

Katherine continued to be indiscreet. Aided by Anne Boleyn's sister-in-law, Viscountess Rochford, Katherine initiated an affair with a man in the King's household, Thomas Culpeper. Katherine's infatuation with Culpeper may have predated her marriage to the King. She presented him with gifts of clothes, ordering him to hide them under his cloak. When Culpeper fell ill, the semi-illiterate Katherine wrote him an indiscreet letter, saying, 'I never longed so much for a thing as I do to see you and to speak with you... it makes my heart die to think what fortune I have that I cannot always be in your company'.[179] Jane Rochford had been smuggling Culpeper into Katherine's rooms late at night, on at least one occasion remaining in the room while they slept together. Other ladies, such as Margaret Morton, were asked to act as lookouts, while other servants carried letters between the pair. The affair continued while they travelled round the country, and whenever they reached a new house, Katherine would immediately seek out a way for Culpeper to make his way to her rooms without being noticed.

On 1 November, Henry publicly stated: 'I render thanks to thee, Oh Lord, that after so many strange accidents that have befallen my marriages, Thou hast been pleased to give me a wife so entirely conformed to my inclinations as her I now have'. But when he returned to his pew, he found a letter from Cranmer. The news was not good.

Information had reached Cranmer of Katherine's previous exploits through one of her former housemates at the Duchess of Norfolk's household, Mary Hall. Although Mary did not know about Katherine's current affair with Culpeper, she did know about her entanglements with Henry Manox and Francis Dereham. Henry was initially reluctant to believe the allegations, but ordered that they should be fully investigated. As time went on and the shock wore off, Henry started to rage against Katherine and his: 'Ill-luck in meeting with such ill-conditioned wives'. The contrast between Henry's current rage and his previous calm when Anne Boleyn was arrested is another indication that Anne was framed with Henry's knowledge and consent.

On 7 November, Katherine was interrogated by a group of councillors. She has typically been portrayed as the most empty headed of Henry's wives but her behaviour under interrogation showed her to be anything but. Despite the fact that her primary concern must have been discovering what the interrogators knew about Culpeper, Katherine withstood their interrogation. She denied all knowledge of any wrongdoings until she realised that she was being questioned only about her past affairs, at which point she made a full confession. Henry was inclined to be merciful, and Katherine would likely have survived, had it not been for Dereham's presence in Katherine's household. There were suspicions that Katherine's affair with him had survived her marriage to Henry, and he was continually interrogated on the subject. Possibly under torture, Dereham revealed that Katherine had replaced him in her affections with Culpeper. In the end, he had sealed both Katherine and Culpeper's fate, without saving himself.

Culpeper and Dereham were executed in December 1541. Culpeper, who had had an adulterous affair with the Queen, had a fairly easy death, being beheaded. Dereham, on the other hand, who had merely slept with an unattached and willing girl, was sentenced to a full traitor's death. He was hanged until he was nearly dead, then cut down, and castrated and disembowelled, before being finally beheaded and quartered. In January 1542, a bill was passed making it treasonable for any woman who married the King not to declare her previous sexual relationships before their marriage, or to assist the Queen to commit adultery. Katherine and her Lady-in-Waiting, Jane Rochford, were finally sentenced to death.

Surprisingly, Katherine had initially been confined in her own rooms at Hampton Court, and then at Syon Abbey. She was finally brought to the Tower of London on 10 February. As she was brought under Tower Bridge on her way, Katherine passed underneath the heads of both Culpeper and Dereham. She asked that the block be brought to her room so that she could practise laying her head on it. On her execution day, she cut a considerably more distinguished figure than Lady Rochford, who had either suffered a mental breakdown or was impersonating a lunatic in the hopes that this might save her from the scaffold. Katherine was probably only 18 years old at the time of her death.

Ironically, Anne of Cleves, the Protestant lady who had been brought to England to cement a Protestant alliance with Germany ended her days as a fervent Catholic. Anne was the last of Henry's wives to die. She died on 16 July 1557, having lived on into the reign of her former stepdaughter and close friend, Mary I. Despite initial problems in securing her full income in the reign of Edward VI, by the end of her life Anne had ensured that her properties were bringing in a comfortable sum and she seems to have been well liked by the people of England. After her death a chronicler, Raphael Holinshed, described her as 'a lady of right commendable regard, courteous, gentle, a good housekeeper and very bountiful to her servants'. In the end, Henry's shortest-lived wife was, perhaps, the most successful.

Notes

1. The World of Marriage

1. Alison Weir, *Henry VIII: King and Court,* (London: Jonathan Cape, 2001), p.96.
2. James Sharpe, 'The Lancaster witches in historical context', in Robert Poole, *The Lancashire Witches: Histories and Stories*, (Manchester: Manchester University Press, 2002), p.3.
3. Claudia Stein, 'The Scientific Revolution', in Beat Kümin (ed.), *The European World*, (Abingdon: Routledge, 2009), p.200.
4. Bernard Capp, 'Gender and Family', in Beat Kümin (ed.), *The European World*, (Abingdon: Routledge, 2009), p.34.
5. Lawrence Stone, *Road to Divorce: A History of the Making and Breaking of Marriage in England,* (Oxford: Oxford University Press, 1992), p.53.

2. Informal Separation: From Living Asunder to Household Captivity

6. John Milton, *The Doctrine and Discipline of Divorce,* (London: 1644).
7. Roderick Philips, *Untying the Knot*, (Cambridge: Cambridge University Press, 1991), p.83.
8. 1570 Norwich Census of the Poor.
9. Lawrence Stone, *Uncertain Union: Marriage in England 1660-1753,* (Oxford: Oxford University Press, 1992), p.232.
10. Bernard Capp, 'Bigamous Marriage in Early Modern England', *The Historical Journal*, Vol.52, No.3, (September 2009), p.542.
11. Lawrence Stone, *Uncertain Unions and Broken Lives,* (Oxford: Oxford University Press, 1995), p.254.
12. Anthony Fletcher, *Gender, Sex and Subordination in Early Modern England,* (New Haven: Yale University Press, 1995), p.145.
13. Fletcher, *Gender, Sex and Subordination in Early Modern England,* pp.166-7.
14. Philips, *Untying the Knot,* p.83.
15. Edwin Brinkworth, *Shakespeare and the Bawdy Court of Stratford,* (Chichester: Phillimore, 1972), p.108.
16. *Churchwardens Presentiments From the Archdeaconry of Chichester 1621-70* from *Ecclesiastical Court Records in the Sussex Record Office,* ed. Hilda Johnstone, (Lewes: Sussex Record Society), XLIX, pp.1-141. (1621-1628).
17. *Churchwardens Presentiments,* ed. Hilda Johnstone, XLIX, p.120.
18. *Churchwardens Presentiments,* ed. Hilda Johnstone, XLIX, p.105.
19. Capp, 'Bigamous Marriage in Early Modern England', p.539.
20. Timothy Stretton, 'Marriage, separation and the common law in England 1540-1660' in Mary Berry and Elizabeth Foyster, *The Family in Early Modern England*, (Cambridge: Cambridge University Press, 2007), p.36.
21. 'Trial of John Cook 30 August 1727'.

170

NOTES

22. 'Trial of Unnamed Woman for Bigamy 14 October 1674', Old Bailey Proceedings Online, April 2012, *http://www.oldbaileyonline.org/browse.jsp?ref=t16741014-4* (16 August 2012).
23. 'Trial of Unnamed Woman for Bigamy 14 October 1674'.
24. 'Trial of Richard Hazlegrove July 1677', Old Bailey Proceedings Online, April 2012, *http://www.oldbaileyonline.org/browse.jsp?ref=t16770711a-6* (16 August 2012).
25. Claire Gervat, *Elizabeth: The Scandalous Life of the Duchess of Kingston*, (London: Random House, 2003), p.84.
26. *The Morning Chronicle and London Advertiser*, Friday 19 April 1776.
27. *Gazeteer and New Daily Advertiser*, Tuesday 16 April 1776.
28. Stone, *Uncertain Unions*, p.248.
29. Parliamentary Archives, House of Lords Papers 1 June 1641 to 5 June 1641, HL/PO/JO/10/1/59, 'Petition of Elizabeth Mullon', 2 June 1641, 59.
30. Lawrence Stone, *Broken Lives: Separation and Divorce in England 1660-1857*, (Oxford: Oxford University Press, 1993), p.68.
31. Bernard Capp, *When Gossips Meet, Women, Family and Neighbourhood in Early Modern England*, (Oxford: Oxford University Press, 2003), p.119.
32. *The Public Adviser*, Volume 15 (31 Aug to 7 Sept 1657), p.272.
33. Capp, *When Gossips Meet*, p.118.
34. *THE TRUE ACCOUNT OF THE BEHAVIOUR AND CONFESSION OF Alice Millikin, Who was Burnt in SMITHFIELD On Wednesday the 2d. of June, 1686. For HIGH-TREASON, in Clipping the Kings Coin*, (London: E Mallet, 1686).
35. Thomas Edwards, *Gangraena*, (London: Ralph Smith, 1646).
36. Capp, *When Gossips Meet*, p.141.
37. Capp, *When Gossips Meet*, p.119.
38. Elizabeth Foyster, 'At the Limits of Liberty: Married Women and Confinement in Eighteenth Century England', *Continuity and Change*, Vol. 17, No. 1, (May 2002), p.56.
39. Foyster, 'At the Limits of Liberty', p.58.

3. Legal Battles: Tricking the Law
40. William Wycherley, *The Plain Dealer*, (London 1677), p.91.
41. Martin Ingram, *Church Courts, Sex and Marriage in England*, 1570-1640, (Cambridge: Cambridge University Press, 1987), p.149.
42. Stone, *Road to Divorce*, p. 202.
43. Stretton, 'Marriage, separation and the common law in England 1540-1660', p.27.
44. National Archives, Court of Requests Records, 'Court Order in the Case of Dame Margery Acton v Sir Robert Acton', REQ/1/9, fo.157.
45. Stretton, 'Marriage, separation and the common law in England 1540-1660', p.28.
46. National Archives, Court of Requests Records, 'Isabell Osmoderley's Bill of Complaint', 7 May 1555, REQ/2/24/82.
47. Patricia Crawford and Laura Gowing, *Women's Worlds in Seventeenth Century England*, (London: Routledge, 2000), p.172.
48. National Archives, Court of Requests Records, 'Isabell Osmoderley's Bill of Complaint', 7 May 1555, REQ/2/24/82.

49. National Archives, Court of Requests records, 'Dame Margery Acton's Bill of Complaint', 27 April 1553, REQ 2/14/53, m.1.
50. Elizabeth Foyster, 'At the Limits of Liberty', p.49.
51. Parliamentary Archives, 11 November 1646, Answer of Elizabeth Walter to petition of William Walter.
52. Miscellaneous Letters, MSS/Additional/23212, 'Undated Letter from Elizabeth Bourne to Anthony Bourne', Letter 14.
53. National Archives, Court of Requests records, 'Parchment Answers', Griffin Jones v Marion Jones et al., 17 April 1594, REQ/2/226/66 m.4.
54. National Archives, Court of Requests records, 'Parchment Replication', Griffin Jones v Marion Jones et al., 3 May 1594, REQ/2/226/66, m.3.
55. National Archives, Court of Requests records, 'Bill of Complaint', Joan Spragin v Martin Spragin et al., 19 November 1595, REQ2/273/67, m.6.
56. National Archives, Court of Requests records, 'Demurrer and Answer', Joan Spragin v Martin Spragin et al., 27 January 1596, REQ2/273/67, m.5.
57. National Archives, Court of Requests records, 'Paper Depositions', Joan Spragin v Martin Spragin et al., 20 May 1598, REQ2/275/80, m.1.
58. National Archives, Court of Requests records, 'Court Order and Decress', Joan Spragin v Martin Spragin et al. 20 May 1598, REQ1/19, p.405.
59. National Archives, Court of Requests records, 'Bill of Complaint', Elizabeth Eggington v Frauncis and John Eggington, 10 January 1609, REQ2/414, 40, m.3.
60. National Archives, Court of Requests records, 'Answer', Elizabeth Eggington v Frauncis and John Eggington, 26 April 1609, REQ2/414/40, m.2.
61. Lambeth Palace, Court of Arches Process Books, 'Blood v Blood', 1704, D.187; Stone, *Uncertain Unions and Broken Lives*, pp.304-314.
62. National Archives, Court of Requests records, 'Rejoinder of Sir Humfrey Stafford', Elizabeth Stafford v Humfrey Stafford, 1562, REQ 2/166/171, m.1.
63. Lambeth Palace Archives, Court of Arches Process Books, 'Middleton v Middleton', 1795, D.1395; Stone, *Uncertain Unions and Broken Lives*, pp.428-513.

4. Separation Agreements: A Disagreeable Situation

64. Hatfield House, 'Last Will and Testament of the Marchioness of Westmeath', 1856, Westmeath Papers.
65. Althorp Papers, MSS/Additional/75513, 'Attested copy of Devise from Robert Poyntz Esq and his Lady to William Poyntz Esquire and others and Deed of Separation', 2 March 1747, Vol. ccxiii.
66. Barrington Letters, MSS/Additional/MS73563, 'Letter from Duchess of Kingston to Earl of Barrington', 19 September 1777, Vol. xviii, Letter 5.
67. Barrington Letters, MSS/Additional/MS73563, 'Letter from Duchess of Kingston to Earl of Barrington', 2 May 1778, Vol. xviii, Letter 31.
68. Barrington Letters, MSS/Additional/MS73563, 'Letter from Duchess of Kingston to Earl of Barrington', 1 August 1777, Vol. xviii, Letter 3.
69. Barrington Letters, MSS/Additional/MS73563, 'Letter from Lord Bristol to Earl of Barrington', 24 Oct 1777, Vol. xviii, Letter 75.

NOTES

70. Lambeth Palace, Process Books of the Court of Arches, Boteler v Boteler, 1675, D.206; Stone; *Uncertain Unions and Broken Lives,* pp. 299-303.
71. Mary Eleanor Bowes, Countess of Strathmore, *Confessions of the Countess of Strathmore*, (London: Locke, 1793).
72. Jesse Foot, *The lives of Andrew Robinson Bowes, Esq. and the Countess of Strathmore, written from thirty-three years professional attendance, from letters, and other well authenticated documents*, (London: Becket and Porter, 1810).
73. George Nugent, Marquess of Westmeath, *A reply to the 'Narrative of the Case of the Marchioness of Westmeath'*, (London, 1857), p.84.
74. Emily Nugent, Marchioness of Westmeath, *A Narrative of the Case of the Marchioness of Westmeath,* (London: James Ridgway, 1857), pp.29-30.
75. Hatfield House, Westmeath Papers, 'Correspondence between the Earl and Countess of Westmeath', September 1817.
76. Lambeth Palace, Court of Arches Process Books, 'Westmeath v Westmeath', 1826, D.2240.
77. Westmeath, *Narrative of the Case of the Marchioness of Westmeath,* pp.141-6.
78. Westmeath, *A Reply to the Narrative of the Marchioness of Westmeath,* p.12.
79. Westmeath, *A Reply to the Narrative of the Marchioness of Westmeath,* p.71.
80. Hatfield, 'Last Will and Testament of Emily Nugent, Marchioness of Westmeath'.
81. Hatfield House, Westmeath Papers, 'Letter of Lady Westmeath to Gerald Wellesley', 28 May 1837.
82. Hatfield House, Westmeath Papers, 'Letter of Lady Westmeath to Lady Rosa Nugent'.
83. Hatfield House, Westmeath Papers, 'Newspaper Clipping', April 1856.

5. Parliamentary Divorces: Adultery on Stage
84. 642, 22 December 1642, Act to Dissolve the Marriage of Henry Duke of Norfolke Earle Marshall of England with the Lady Mary Mordaunt and to enable the Duke to marry again.
85. Stuart Anderson, 'Legislative Divorce, Law For the Aristocracy?' in G.R. Grubin & D. Sugarman, *Law Economy and Society 1780-1914: Essays in the History of English Law*, (Abingdon: Professional Books, 1984), p.414.
86. Crawford and Mendelson, *Women in Early Modern England,* p.147.
87. Lambeth Palace, Court of Arches Process Books, 'Calvert v Calvert', D355, 1710.
88. Lambeth Palace, Court of Arches Process Books, 'Beaufort v Beaufort', D137, 1742.
89. 'Calvert v Calvert', D355.
90. Beaufort v Beaufort, D137.
91. Calvert v Calvert, D355.
92. Beaufort v Beaufort, D137.
93. Beaufort v Beaufort, D137.
94. Stone, *Broken Lives,* p.121.
95. Beaufort v Beaufort, D137.
96. *Broken Lives*, p.341.
97. Suffolk Record Office, Grafton Family Papers, 1768, HA/513/4/86.

98. *Broken Lives*, p.341.
99. Beaufort v Beaufort, D137.
100. House of Lords Papers 10 January 1698-17 January 1698, HL/PO/JO/10/1/496/1197, 'Witness Cross-Examinations in the Divorce Trial of the Earl and Countess of Macclesfield', 21 January to 18 February 1698, 1197(e).
101. House of Lords Papers 12 January 1692, HL/PO/JO/10/1/443/524, D. Norfolk's Divorce Bill, 'What the Duke of Norfolk's witnesses said at the Bar in answer to the questions asked them by the Duchess's Proctor before the swearing them', 23 January 1691, 524(o).
102. House of Lords Papers 10 January 1698-17 January 1698, HL/PO/JO/10/1/496/1197, 'Witness Cross-Examination of Olive Mounteney and William Banastre', 18 February 1698, 1197(e26).
103. House of Lords Papers 10 January 1698 to 17 January 1698, HL/PO/JO/10/1/496/1197, 'Witness Cross-Examination of Margaret Davis', 16 February 1698, 1197(e24).
104. Crawford and Mendelson, *Women in Early Modern England*, p.43.
105. Philips, *Untying the Knot*, p.66.
106. Anderson, 'Legislative Divorce, Law For the Aristocracy?', p. 423.
107. House of Lords Papers 10 January 1698-17 January 1698, HL/PO/JO/10/1/496/1197, 'Petition of Anne Countess of Macclesfield', 28 February 1698, 1197(j).
108. House of Lords Papers 12 January 1692, HL/PO/JO/10/1/443/524, D. Norfolk's Divorce Bill, 'Petition of Mary Duchess of Norfolk', 8 January 1691, 524(a).
109. House of Lords Papers 12 January 1692, HL/PO/JO/10/1/443/524, D. Norfolk's Divorce Bill, 'Petition of Mary Duchess of Norfolk', 8 January 1691, 524(a).
110. House of Lords Papers 12 January 1692, HL/PO/JO/10/1/443/524, D. Norfolk's Divorce Bill, 'List of Witnesses to be Summoned on Behalf of the Duke', 22 January 1691, 524(i).
111. House of Lords Papers 12 January 1692, HL/PO/JO/10/1/443/524, D. Norfolk's Divorce Bill, 'Petition of Mary Duchess of Norfolk',13 January 1692, 524(b).
112. House of Lords Papers 12 January 1692, HL/PO/JO/10/1/443/524, D. Norfolk's Divorce Bill, 'Answer of Mary Duchess of Norfolk to the Charge Exhibited Against her by the Duke of Norfolk Before the Lords Spiritual and Temporal in Parliament Assembled', 19 January 1691, 524(e).
113. House of Lords Papers 12 January 1692, HL/PO/JO/10/1/443/524, D. Norfolk's Divorce Bill, 'Answer of Mary Duchess of Norfolk', 25 January 1692, 524(h).
114. House of Lords Papers 12 January 1692, HL/PO/JO/10/1/443/524, D. Norfolk's Divorce Bill, 'Answer of Mary Duchess of Norfolk', 25 January 1692, 524(h).
115. Stone, *Road to Divorce*, p.317.
116. House of Lords Papers (Large Parchments), HL/PO/JO/10/3/270/53, 14 May 1777 to 11 March 1778, Blake's Divorce Bill, 'Petition and Bill of Sir Patrick Blake, Bt', 10 March 1778, 53.
117. House of Lords Papers (Large Parchments), HL/PO/JO/10/3/270/53, 14 May 1777 to 11 March 1778, Blake's Divorce Bill, 'Petition and Bill of Sir Patrick Blake, Bt', 10 March 1778, 53.

118. British Library, Lamb Papers, 'Letter of Georgiana, Duchess of Devonshire to Lady Melbourne', 20 November 1791, MSS/Additional/45911.
119. Grafton Family Papers, HA 513/4/94.
120. Caroline Norton, *The Law Relating to the Custody of Infants,* (London: Roake and Varty, 1838, p.1).
121. Norton, *The Law Relating to the Custody of Infants,* p.30.
122. Mary Delany, *The Autobiography and Correspondence of Mary Granville, Mrs Delany,* Vol. Two, (London: R Bentley, 1862), p.465.
123. Society of Antiquaries of London, 'Letter of Lord Bolingbroke to Maria, Lady Waldegrave', MS 444/18/22, 31 August 1765.
124. Ilchester, Countess of and Stavordale, Lord (eds), *The Life and Letters of Lady Sarah Lennox, 1745-1826* (London: J Murray, 1901).
125. C Barrett (ed.), *The Diary and Letters of Madame D'Arblay 1778-1840, as edited by her neice, with preface and notes by Austin Dobson,* Vol. Two, (London: 1904), p.91.

6. Wife Sales: Disgraceful Transactions

126. *The Times,* 26 April 1832.
127. Samuel Menefee, *Wives For Sale,* (Oxford: Basil Blackwell, 1981), pp.70-72.
128. Sabine Baring Goulding, *Devonshire Characters and Strange Events,* (London: Bodley Head, 1908), pp.59-60.
129. Menefee, *Wives For Sale,* p.34.
130. Hufton, *The Prospect Before Her,* p.259.
131. E. P. Thompson, *Customs in Common,* (Merlin, 1991), p.411.
132. Thompson, *Customs in Common,* p.411
133. Elizabeth Chudleigh, *The Laws Respecting Women,* (London: Johnson, 1777).
134. *Manchester Mercury,* 12 October 1819.
135. Menefee, *Wives For Sale,* p.273.
136. Menefee, *Wives For Sale,* p.102.
137. *The Times,* 26 April 1832.
138. *The Buckinghamshire Herald,* 16 May 1846.
139. *Jackson's Oxford Journal,* 13 August 1796.
140. *A True and Singular Account of Wife Selling,* (Gateshead: W. Stephenson, 1822).
141. Menefee, *Wives For Sale,* p.58.
142. Menefee, *Wives For Sale,* p.71.
143. *Worcester Chronicle,* 22 July 1857.
144. Thompson, *Customs in Common,* p.451.
145. *The Times,* 3 February 1837.
146. *Particular And Merry Account Of A Most Entertaining And Curious Sale Of A Wife,* (Birmingham, 1856).
147. Chudleigh, *The Laws Respecting Women,* p.55.
148. Menefee, *Wives For Sale,* p.53 and p.63.
149. *Morning Chronicle and London Advertiser,* 14 January 1815.
150. Thompson, *Customs in Common,* p.435.
151. *Northern Star,* 17 May 1851.

152. *The Times*, 29 August 1833.
153. *The Kingdomes Weekly Intelligencer,* 1642.
154. *The Annual Register 1766,* (London: J. Dodsley, 1793).
155. *Glasgow Herald,* 10 November 1856.
156. *Account of the Sale of a Wife.* Anon.
157. *Jackson's Oxford Journal,* 28 April 1810.
158. *http://www.berkshirehistory.com/legends/chandos.html*
159. *Manchester Gazette,* 26 June 1824.
160. *Exeter and Plymouth Chronicle,* 24 Jan 1846.
161. *The Times,* 26 April 1832.
162. *Preston Chronicle,* 28 July 1849.
163. *Leicester Journal,* 7 May 1852.
164. *Carlisle Patriot,* 21 August 1819.
165. *Morning Post,* 1 September 1845.
166. *Stamford Mercury,* 12 February 1819.

Appendix. The Divorces of Henry VIII: The Sharp'st Kind of Justice

167. Giles Tremlett, *Catherine of Aragon: Henry's Spanish Queen,* (Faber and Faber, 2011), p. 89.
168. William Shakespeare, '*Henry VIII*', *The Complete Works of William Shakespeare,* (London: Hamlyn, 1983), p.609.
169. Calendar of State Papers, Foreign, Elizabeth, Volume One, September 1559, 'Letter from Alexander Ales to the Queen', p.527.
170. 'Letter of Sir William Kingston to Thomas Cromwell', from Original Letters Indicative of British History, Sir Henry Ellis (ed). (London: Harding, Triphook and Lehard, 1825), p.55.
171. 'Letter of Sir William Kingston to Thomas Cromwell', p.56.
172. Charles Wriothesley, *A Chronicle Of England During The Reigns Of The Tudors, From A.D. 1485 To 1559,* (London: J.B. Nichols and Sons, 1875).
173. 'Cromwell's Letter to the King Concerning His Marriage With Ann of Cleves', from The History of the Reformation of the Church of England, Volume IV, Gilbert Burnet, (ed). (New York: D. Appleton, 1843), p.110.
174. 'Deposition of Mr Doctor Butts', *Ecclesiastical Memorials,* John Strype (ed.), (Oxford: Clarendon Press, 1822), p.461.
175. 'Such Communication as was between the Queen's Grace and the Ladies of Rutland, Rochford and Edgcombe', *Ecclesiastical Memorials,* Strype (ed.) pp.462-3.
176. Letters and Papers of the Reign of Henry VIII, Volume XV, 11 July 1540 'Letter of Anne of Cleves to Henry VIII', Item 925.
177. Calendar of State Papers, Spanish, Volume VI I (1538-1542), pp.306-6.
178. Historical Manuscripts Commission Bath, 5 vols. (London, 1904-80), II, pp.8-9.
179. National Archives, State Papers of Henry VIII, 'Letter of Katherine Howard to Thomas Culpeper', SP 1/167.

Bibliography

Manuscript Sources
British Library
- Barrington Letters, MSS/Additional/MS73563, 'Letters from the Duchess of Kingston to the Earl of Barrington', 1777-8, Vol. xviii.
- Althorp Papers, MSS/Additional/75513, Papers relating to Robert Poyntz's separation from his wife and settlement of his estate; 1748, Vol. ccxiii.
- 'Miscellaneous letters and papers relating principally to disputes between Anthony Bourne and his wife, Elizabeth', MSS/Additional/23212.

Lambeth Palace Archives: Records of the Court of Arches
- Process Books of the Court of Arches 1675, D.206, Boteler v. Boteler.
- Process Books of the Court of Arches 1704, D.187, Blood v. Blood.
- Process Books of the Court of Arches 1710, D.355, Calvert v. Calvert.
- Process Books of the Court of Arches 1742, D.137, Beaufort v. Beaufort.
- Process Books of the Court of Arches 1796, D.1395, Middleton v. Middleton.
- Process Books of the Court of Arches 1826, D.2240, Westmeath v. Westmeath.

Parliamentary Archives
- House of Lords Papers 1 June 1641 – 5 June 1641, HL/PO/JO/10/1/59, 'Petition of Elizabeth Mullon', 2 June 1641, 59.
- House of Lords Papers, 8 Mar 1644-24 Oct 1648, HL/PO/JO/10/1/59, Answer of Elizabeth Walter to petition of William Walter, 11 November 1646.
- House of Lords Papers 12 January 1692, HL/PO/JO/10/1/443/524, D. Norfolk's Divorce Bill, 'An Act to Dissolve the Marriage of the Duke of Norfolk and the Lady Mary Mordaunt, 12 January 1692, 524.
- House of Lords Papers 12 January 1692, HL/PO/JO/10/1/443/524, D. Norfolk's Divorce Bill, 'Petition of Mary Duchess of Norfolk', 8 January 1692, 524(a).
- House of Lords Papers 12 January 1692, HL/PO/JO/10/1/443/524, D. Norfolk's Divorce Bill, 'Petition of Mary Duchess of Norfolk', 13 January 1692, 524(b).
- House of Lords Papers 12 January 1692, HL/PO/JO/10/1/443/524, D. Norfolk's Divorce Bill, 'The usual method of proceeding in the Ecclesiastical Courts when a man sues his wife in a cause of separation or divorce for adultery', 16 January 1692, 524(c).
- House of Lords Papers 12 January 1692, HL/PO/JO/10/1/443/524, D. Norfolk's Divorce Bill, 'Answer of Mary Duchess of Norfolk to the Charge Exhibited Against her by the Duke of Norfolk Before the Lords Spiritual and Temporal in Parliament Assembled', 19 January 1692, 524(e).
- House of Lords Papers 12 January 1692, HL/PO/JO/10/1/443/524, D. Norfolk's

Divorce Bill, 'Answer of Mary Duchess of Norfolk', 25 January 1692, 524(h).
- House of Lords Papers 12 January 1692, HL/PO/JO/10/1/443/524, D. Norfolk's Divorce Bill, 'List of Witnesses to be Summoned on Behalf of the Duke', 22 January 1692, 524(i).
- House of Lords Papers 12 January 1692, HL/PO/JO/10/1/443/524, D. Norfolk's Divorce Bill, 'Duchess of Norfolk's Letter to the House of Lords', 23 January 1692, 524(l).
- House of Lords Papers, 12 January 1692, HL/PO/JO/10/1/443/524, D. Norfolk's Divorce Bill, 'What the Duke of Norfolk's witnesses said at the Bar in answer to the questions asked them by the Duchess's Proctor before the swearing them', 23 January 1692, 524(o).
- House of Lords Papers 10 January 1698-17 January 1698, HL/PO/JO/10/1/496/1197, 'Draft Act for Dissolving the Marriage Between Charles Earl of Macclesfield and Anne his wife and to illegitimate the Children of the Said Anne', 15 January 1698, 1197.
- House of Lords Papers 10 January 1698-17 January 1698, HL/PO/JO/10/1/496/1197, 'Petition of Anne Countess of Macclesfield', 14 February 1698, 1197(d).
- House of Lords Papers 10 January 1698-17 January 1698, HL/PO/JO/10/1/496/1197, 'Witness Cross-Examination of Dinah Allsup', 21 January 1698, 1197(e1).
- House of Lords Papers 10 January 1698-17 January 1698, HL/PO/JO/10/1/496/1197, 'Witness Cross-Examination of Margaret Davis', 16 February 1698, 1197(e24).
- House of Lords Papers 10 January 1698-17 January 1698, HL/PO/JO/10/1/496/1197, 'Witness Cross-Examination of Olive Mounteney and William Banastre', 18 February 1698, 1197(e26).
- House of Lords Papers 10 January 1698-17 January 1698, HL/PO/JO/10/1/496/1197, 'Petition of Anne Countess of Macclesfield', 28 February 1698, 1197(j).
- House of Lords Papers 31 March 1698 to 13 December 1698, HL/PO/JO/10/1/493, Knight Divorce Act, 'Petition of Mary Watkinson and Thomas Goodinge the Younger', 9 April 1698, 1158.
- House of Lords Papers 1715 to 6 May 1715, HL/PO/JO/10/6/253, Downing Divorce Bill, 'Petition of Mary Forester Regarding the Downing Divorce Bill', 26 April 1715, 3873(a).
- House of Lords Papers (Large Parchments), HL/PO/JO/10/3/262, 1 Feb 1771 to 30 Jan 1772, 'Bill to dissolve the marriage of Viscount Ligonier to Penelope Pitt', 27 January 1772, 43.
- House of Lords Papers (Large Parchments), HL/PO/JO/10/3/270/53, 14 May 1777 to 11 March 1778, Blake's Divorce Bill, 'Petition and Bill of Sir Patrick Blake, Bt', 10 March 1778, 53.

The National Archives – Archives of the Court of Requests
- National Archives, Court of Requests Records, 'Court Order in the Case of Dame Margery Acton v Sir Robert Acton', 22 June 1553, REQ/1/9, fo.157.
- National Archives, Court of Requests Records, 'Isabell Osmoderley's Bill of Complaint', 7 May 1555, REQ/2/24/82.
- National Archives, Court of Requests records, 'Dame Margery Acton's Bill of

BIBLIOGRAPHY

Complaint', 27 April 1553, REQ 2/14/53, m.1.
* National Archives, Court of Requests records, 'Rejoinder of Sir Humfrey Stafford', Elizabeth Stafford v Humfrey Stafford, 1562, REQ 2/166/171, m.1.
* National Archives, Court of Requests records, 'Parchment Answers', Griffin Jones v Marion Jones et al., 17 April 1594, REQ/2/226/66 m.4.
* National Archives, Court of Requests records, 'Parchment Answers', Griffin Jones v Marion Jones et al., 17 April 1594, REQ/2/226/66 m.4.
* National Archives, Court of Requests records, 'Parchment Replication', Griffin Jones v Marion Jones et al., 3 May 1594, REQ/2/226/66, m.3.
* National Archives, Court of Requests records, 'Bill of Complaint', Joan Spragin v Martin Spragin et al., 19 November 1595, REQ2/273/67, m.6.
* National Archives, Court of Requests records, 'Demurrer and Answer', Joan Spragin v Martin Spragin et al., 27 January 1596, REQ2/273/67, m.5.
* National Archives, Court of Requests records, 'Paper Depositions', Joan Spragin v Martin Spragin et al., 20 May 1598, REQ2/275/80, m.1.
* National Archives, Court of Requests records, 'Court Order and Decress', Joan Spragin v Martin Spragin et al. 20 May 1598, REQ1/19, p.405.
* National Archives, Court of Requests records, 'Bill of Complaint', Elizabeth Eggington v Frauncis and John Eggington, 10 January 1609, REQ2/414, 40, m.3.
* National Archives, Court of Requests records, 'Answer', Elizabeth Eggington v. Frauncis and John Eggington, 26 April 1609, REQ2/414/40, m.2.

The National Archives – Other Papers
* National Archives, State Papers of Henry VIII, 'Letter of Katherine Howard to Thomas Culpeper', SP 1/167.

Oxfordshire Record Office
* Edwin Brinkworth, *The 'Bawdy Court' of Banbury: The Act Book of the Peculiar Court of Banbury 1625-1638,* (Banbury: The Banbury Historical Society, 1997).

West Sussex Record Office
* *Churchwardens Presentiments From the Archdeaconry of Chichester 1621-70,* from *Ecclesiastical Court Records in the Sussex Record Office,* ed. Hilda Johnstone, (Lewes: Sussex Record Society), XLIX.
* *Churchwardens Presentiments from the Archdeaconry of Lewes 1674,* from *Ecclesiastical Court Records Held by the Sussex Record Office,* ed. Hilda Johnstone (Lewes: Sussex Record Society), L.

Hatfield House
* *Westmeath Papers.*

Newspapers and Periodicals
* *The Kingdomes Weekly Intelligencer,* 1642.
* *The Public Adviser*, Volume 15 (31 Aug-7 Sept 1657).
* *THE TRUE ACCOUNT OF THE BEHAVIOUR AND CONFESSION OF Alice*

Millikin, Who was Burnt in SMITHFIELD On Wednesday the 2d. of June, 1686. For HIGH-TREASON, in Clipping the Kings Coin, (London: E Mallet, 1686).
* *Gazeteer and New Daily Advertiser*, Tuesday 16 April 1776.
* *The Morning Chronicle and London Advertiser,* Friday 19 April 1776.
* *The Annual Register 1766,* (London: J. Dodsley, 1793).
* *Jackson's Oxford Journal,* 13 August 1796.
* *Morning Chronicle and London Advertiser,* 14 January 1815.
* *Carlisle Patriot,* 21 August 1819.
* *Manchester Mercury,* 12 October 1819.
* *Manchester Gazette*, 26 June 1824.
* *A True and Singular Account of Wife Selling,* (Gateshead: W. Stephenson, 1822).
* *Times,* 26 April 1832.
* *Times,* 29 August 1833.
* *Times,* 3 February 1837.
* *Morning Post,* 1 September 1845.
* *Exeter and Plymouth Chronicle,* 24 Jan 1846.
* *The Buckinghamshire Herald,* 16 May 1846.
* *Preston Chronicle*, 28 July 1849.
* *Northern Star*, 17 May 1851.
* *Particular And Merry Account Of A Most Entertaining And Curious Sale Of A Wife,* (Birmingham, 1856).
* *Leicester Journal*, 7 May 1852.
* *Glasgow Herald*, 10 November 1856.
* *Worcester Chronicle,* 22 July 1857.

Contemporary Books, Articles, Pamphlets and Speeches
* Chudleigh, Elizabeth, *The Laws Respecting Women*, (London: Johnson, 1777).
* Edwards, Thomas, *Gangraena,* (London: Ralph Smith, 1646).
* Delany, Mary, *The Autobiography and Correspondence of Mary Granville, Mrs Delany*, Volume Two, (London: R Bentley, 1862).
* Foot, Jesse, *The lives of Andrew Robinson Bowes, Esq. and the Countess of Strathmore, written from thirty-three years professional attendance, from letters, and other well authenticated documents,* (London: Becket and Porter, 1810).
* Ilchester, Countess of and Stavordale, Lord (eds), *The Life and Letters of Lady Sarah Lennox, 1745-1826* (London: J Murray, 1901).
* Milton, John, *The Doctrine and Discipline of Divorce,* (London, 1643).
* Norton, Caroline, *The Separation of Mother and Child by the Law of "Custody of Infants" Considered*, (London: Roake and Varty, 1838).
* Norton, Caroline, *A Plain Letter to the Lord Chancellor on the Infant Custody Bill,* (London, James Ridgway, 1839).
* Norton, Caroline, *A Letter To The Queen On Lord Chancellor Cranworth's Marriage And Divorce Bill,* (London: Longman, Brown, Green and Longmans, 1855).
* Philips, Con, *An Apology For the Conduct of Mrs Teresia Constantia Philips,* (London, 1748).
* Shakespeare, William, *'Henry VIII'*, *The Complete Works of William Shakespeare,*

BIBLIOGRAPHY

(London: Hamlyn, 1983).
- Strathmore, Mary Eleanor Bowes, Countess of, *Confessions of the Countess of Strathmore,* (London: Locke, 1793).
- Westmeath, Emily Nugent, Marchioness of, *Narrative of the Case of the Marchioness of Westmeath,* (London: James Ridgway, 1857).
- Westmeath, George Nugent, Marquess of, *A reply to the "Narrative of the case of the Marchioness of Westmeath",* (London, 1857).
- Wriothesley, Charles, *A Chronicle Of England During The Reigns Of The Tudors, From A.D. 1485 To 1559,* (London: J.B. Nichols and Sons, 1875).
- Wycherley, William, *The Plain Dealer,* (London, 1677).

Edited Primary Sources
- Calendar of State Papers, Foreign, Elizabeth, Volume One, September 1559, 'Letter from Alexander Ales to the Queen'.
- Letter of Sir William Kingston to Thomas Cromwell, from Original Letters Indicative of British History, Sir Henry Ellis (ed). (London: Harding, Triphook and Lehard, 1825.)
- Cromwell's Letter to the King Concerning His Marriage With Anne of Cleve, from *The History of the Reformation of the Church of England,* Volume IV, Gilbert Burnet, (ed). (New York: D. Appleton, 1843.)
- Deposition of Mr Doctor Butts, *Ecclesiastical Memorials,* John Strype (ed.), (Oxford: Clarendon Press, 1822.)
- 'Such Communication as was between the Queen's Grace and the Ladies of Rutland, Rochford and Edgcombe', *Ecclesiastical Memorials,* Strype (ed.)
- Letters and Papers of the Reign of Henry VIII, Volume XV, 11 July 1540 'Letter of Anne of Cleves to Henry VIII', Item 925.

Published Secondary Sources
- Anderson, Stuart, 'Legislative Divorce, Law For the Aristocracy?' in G.R. Grubin & D. Sugarman, *Law Economy and Society 1780-1914: Essays in the History of English Law,* (Abingdon: Professional Books, 1984), pp.412-44.
- Atkinson, Diane, *The Criminal Conversation of Mrs Norton,* (London: Preface, 2012).
- Bailey, Joanne, *Unquiet Lives, Marriage and Marital Breakdown in England 1660-1800,* (Cambridge: Cambridge University Press, 2003).
- Capp, Bernard, *When Gossips Meet: Women, Family and Neighbourhood in Early Modern England,* (Oxford: Oxford University Press, 2003).
- Capp, Bernard, Bigamous Marriage in Early Modern England', *The Historical Journal,* Vol.52, No.3, (September 2009).
- Crawford, Patricia and Gowing, Laura, *Women's Worlds in Seventeenth Century England,* (London: Routledge, 2000).
- Crawford, Patricia & Mendelson, Sara, *Women in Early Modern England 1550-1720,* (Oxford: Oxford University Press, 1998).
- Fletcher, Anthony, *Gender, Sex and Subordination in Early Modern England: 1500-1800,* (New Haven: Yale University Press, 1995).

- Foyster, Elizabeth *Manhood in Early Modern England: Honour, Sex and Marriage,* (London: Longman, 1999).
- Foyster, Elizabeth, 'At the Limits of Liberty: Married Women and Confinement in Eighteenth Century England', *Continuity and Change*, Vol. 17, No.1, (May 2002), pp.39-62.
- Baring-Gould, Sabine, *Devonshire Characters and Strange Events*, (London: Bodley Head, 1908)
- Gervat, Claire, *Elizabeth: The Scandalous Life of the Duchess of Kingston,* (London: Random House, 2003).
- Helmholz, Richard, *The Oxford History of the Laws of England*, 11 vols, (Oxford: Oxford University Press, 2004) Vol.6 1483-1558.
- Heal, Felicity and Holmes, Clive, *The Gentry in England and Wales 1500-1700,* (Basingstoke: Macmillan Press, 1994).
- Hicks, Carola, *Improper Pursuits: The Scandalous Life of Lady Di Beauclerk,* (Basingstoke: Macmillan, 2001).
- Houlbrooke, Ralph, *The English Family: 1450-1700,* (London: Longman, 1984).
- Hufton, Olwen, *The Prospect Before Her: A History of Women in Western Europe 1500-1800,* (New York: Random House, 1995).
- Martin, Ingram, *Church Courts, Sex and Marriage in England 1570-1640,* (Cambridge: Cambridge University Press, 1987).
- McSheffrey, Shannon, *Marriage, sex and civic culture in late medieval London,* (Philadelphia: University of Philadelphia Press, 2006).
- Menefee, Samuel *Wives For Sale: An ethnographic study of English popular divorce,* (Oxford: Blackwell, 1981).
- Moore, Wendy, *Wedlock: How Georgian Britain's Worst Husband Met His Match,* (London: Phoenix, 2010).
- O'Hara, Diana, *Courtship and Constraint: Rethinking the Making of Marriage in Tudor England,* (Manchester: Manchester University Press).
- Ozment, Steven, *When Fathers Ruled: Family Life in Reformation Europe,* (Cambridge: Harvard University Press, 1983).
- Philips, Roderick, *Putting Asunder: A History of Divorce in Western Society,* (Cambridge: Cambridge University Press, 1988).
- Philips, Roderick, *Untying the Knot: A Short History of Divorce,* (Cambridge: Cambridge University Press, 1991).
- Sharpe, James, 'The Lancaster witches in historical context', in Poole, Robert, *The Lancashire Witches: Histories and Stories*, (Manchester: Manchester University Press, 2002).
- Shephard, Alexandra, *Meanings of Manhood in Early Modern England,* (Oxford: Oxford University Press, 2003).
- Starkey, David, *Six Wives: The Queens of Henry VIII,* (London: Chatto and Windus, 2003).
- Stone, Lawrence, *Broken Lives: Separation and Divorce in England 1660-1857,* (Oxford: Oxford University Press, 1993).
- Stone, Lawrence, *The Family, Sex and Marriage in England 1500-1800*, (London: Penguin, 1990).

BIBLIOGRAPHY

- Stone, Lawrence, *Road to Divorce: A History of the Making and Breaking of Marriage in England,* (Oxford: Oxford University Press, 1992).
- Stone, Lawrence, *Uncertain Union: Marriage in England 1660-1753,* (Oxford: Oxford University Press, 1992).
- Stretton, Timothy, 'Marriage, separation and the common law in England 1540-1660' in Berry, Mary and Foyster, Elizabeth, *The Family in Early Modern England,* (Cambridge: Cambridge University Press, 2007).
- Thomas, Keith, 'Women in the Civil War Sects', *Past & Present,* No. 13 (Apr. 1958), pp.42-62.
- Thompson, E.P., *Customs in Common,* (London: Merlin, 1991).
- Tremlett, Giles, *Catherine of Aragon: Henry's Spanish Queen,* (Faber and Faber).
- Vickery, Amanda, *Behind Closed Doors: At Home in Georgian England,* (New Haven: Yale University Press, 2009).
- Weir, Alison, *The Six Wives of Henry VIII,* (London: Random House, 1991).
- Weir, Alison, *Henry VIII: King and Court,* (London: Jonathan Cape, 2001).
- Wolfram, Sybil, 'Divorce in England 1700-1857', *Oxford Journal of Legal Studies,* Vol.5 No.2, (1985), pp.155-186.

Online Sources
- 'Trial of John Cook 30th August 1727', Old Bailey Proceedings Online, April 2012, *http://www.oldbaileyonline.org* (16th August 2012).
- 'Trial of Unnamed Woman for Bigamy 14th October 1674', Old Bailey Proceedings Online, April 2012, *http://www.oldbaileyonline. org* (16th August 2012).
- 'Trial of Richard Hazlegrove July 1677', Old Bailey Proceedings Online, April 2012, *http://www.oldbaileyonline.org* (16th August 2012).

Index

INDEX

INDEX

INDEX